A Step-by-Step Approach to Writing the Feature Film Screenplay

JOHN P. VOURLIS

understanding
SCREENWRITING

Kendall Hunt
publishing company

Cover image © Shutterstock.com

publishing company

www.kendallhunt.com
Send all inquiries to:
4050 Westmark Drive
Dubuque, IA 52004-1840

ISBN: 978-1-5249-6896-0

Published in the United States of America

Table of Contents

Foreword

If you are an aspiring screenwriter, this book will prove indispensable. It will save you countless hours of trial and error, countless rewrites and yet more rewrites. Not that the book will entirely eliminate rewriting, because as John Vourlis points out, creative writing should really be called creative rewriting. But there's no question that *Understanding Screenwriting* will make the writing process easier, permitting you to approach the craft of screenwriting with greater confidence and far fewer missteps.

Vourlis generously acknowledges the contributions of his predecessors, like Syd Field, Blake Snyder, Frank Daniel and others, all of whom employ the three-act structure, derived from stage writing. Vourlis refines many of the ideas of these predecessors and offers his own formula: 1 (concept), 3 (acts), 8 (sequences), 16 (story beats), 40 (scenes) as a template for constructing an effective cinematic structure.

"Formula" is often employed as a negative term by critics. Characters and plots are dismissed as "formulaic," meaning they are constructed according to a clichéd mechanical concept, devoid of creativity or originality. The truth of the matter, of course, is that all writing is formulaic to some extent, depending on the genre. A Shakespearean sonnet, for example, consists of 14 intricately rhymed lines, irrespective of the poem's content. On the other hand, Walt Whitman's *Leaves of Grass* is written in free verse, with relatively little patterning. In fact, even Whitman's epic poem is patterned, but less rigorously than a tight structure like a sonnet.

Stage and screen writing is relatively formulaic in terms of structure. That is, the narrative is patterned according to a set of time-honored conventions. Not all plays and movies adhere to these conventions, but most of them do. Vourlis is flexible about the use of his formula: It's not etched in stone. But, by analyzing the structural patterns of such mainstream movies as *The Wizard of Oz, Dallas Buyers Club, Raiders of the Lost Ark, Legally Blonde,* and *Get Out* he demonstrates how all of these movies employ a similar dramatic structure. Vourlis is fond of the phrase "new wine poured into old bottles," meaning that the original component of screenwriting (new wine) is structured into a predetermined pattern (old bottles).

Step by step, Vourlis takes the reader from the inception of a concept to its segmentation into a pattern that is most likely to engage the audience's emotional involvement. His emphasis is not on "creativity," which after all is unique to each writer, but on how this creative content is broken down into interrelated units that form a coherent and satisfying dramatic structure.

But wait, there's more. The book is also filled with helpful tips in dealing with typical problems that confront the screenwriter. Vourlis also suggests other books that augment his own ideas. He presents the reader with a variety of exercises that can help the beginning screenwriter see how the 1-3-8-16-40 formula underlines most commercial films. Furthermore, Vourlis' book is very clearly written, with a minimum of jargon and technical terms. In addition, he demonstrates how all professional screenplays should be formatted, offering specific requirements that make a screenplay look professional.

I wish I had this book, or one like it, when I was an aspiring playwright at the famous Iowa Writers Workshop. It would have saved me a lot of time, sweat, and frustration. The excellent teachers at the Workshop taught me many of the same ideas that are contained within these covers, but it took me years to assimilate them. They're available to you here in a much more convenient format.

~**Louis Giannetti,** Professor Emeritus of English and Film, Case Western Reserve University, and author of ***Understanding Movies***

Acknowledgments

I have been studying film, especially screenwriting, for the better part of three decades, and I've tried to learn something from every book, teacher, fellow writer, and colleague I've encountered on this journey. Their names are many, and I will herein acknowledge a few: Aristotle, Lajos Egri, Syd Field, Paul Lucey, Frank Daniel, Robert McKee, David Freeman, and Blake Snyder. I had the pleasure of meeting several of these great minds, and I have learned much from all of them and their works on writing. They are all giants, and I owe all of them a deep bow of gratitude.

To a few folks I've met along the way, special thanks are in order.

First and foremost, is Louis Giannetti. I met Lou when I was an undergraduate student in his *Introduction to Film* class at Case Western Reserve University in Cleveland, Ohio, way back when. That class and his book, *Understanding Movies*, proved to be the Rosetta Stone of my life. Everything in my life after that encounter came into focus slowly but surely, leading up to the almost surreal day of writing my own book, with a foreword from the man himself. Words cannot express the deep gratitude I feel for knowing Dr. Giannetti, first as a teacher, then as a mentor, and these days as a trusted friend. My life would have been very different had I not met you, sir.

To all the screenwriters of the works I have referenced in this book, I am grateful. You have all inspired me, as well as countless screenwriters and multitudes of moviegoers with your exceptional work. Thank you.

I am also very grateful to my former colleague at Cleveland State, Brian Johnson for pointing me in the right direction when I decided to write this book. And I am deeply grateful to my current Cleveland State colleague, Sal Cardoni, whose keen eye and thoughtful critiques have left this a better book than when I started; as well as to my screenwriting pal and fellow USC film school alum Shonna Diskin-Kline, who gave me a much appreciated working writer's view of this project.

To all the good folks at Kendall Hunt who've made this book possible, including Sean Skinner and Paige Timm, I am also sincerely grateful.

I'd also be deeply remiss if I did not thank all my CSU screenwriting students, especially Anthony Taylor for the generous use of some of his student work, and Alec Greenwald and Andrew Robinson for giving me a screenwriting student's perspective on the book. I've learned as much about screenwriting as a teacher as I have as a student, and so to all my students, I say thank you.

And finally, I need to extend a sincere thank you to my CSU colleagues George Ray & Evan Lieberman, two of the finest people I know. Without them I would never have discovered the joys of teaching or publishing. That is a debt that can never be repaid, gentlemen. Thank you.

A Note Before You Begin

Before you get started, I strongly suggest you watch as many of the movies listed below as time permits. If you can only watch a few, make sure you view RAIDERS OF THE LOST ARK, LEGALLY BLONDE, THE SECRET LIFE OF WALTER MITTY (2013), DALLAS BUYERS CLUB, and GET OUT; they are all heavily referenced throughout this book and so a familiarity with them will be extremely valuable to you. These films were chosen because they illustrate a wide variety of genres, as well as different eras, in Hollywood screenwriting. All these movies can be found on streaming services such as Netflix or on DVD at your local library. Where possible, you should also read the scripts for as many of these films as you can. Look for the latest revisions or shooting scripts which can be found through various internet resources; search the titles online to find them.

Movie Reference List:

- THE WIZARD OF OZ, screenplay by Noel Langley, Florence Ryerson, and Edgar Allan Woolf, based on the novel *The Wonderful Wizard of Oz* by L. Frank Baum
- RAIDERS OF THE LOST ARK, screenplay by Lawrence Kasdan, based on a story by George Lucas and Philip Kaufman
- SPEED, screenplay by Graham Yost and Joss Whedon (uncredited)
- DIE HARD, screenplay by Jeb Stuart and Steven E. de Souza, based on the novel *Nothing Lasts Forever* by Roderick Thorp
- WHEN HARRY MET SALLY, screenplay by Nora Ephron
- LEGALLY BLONDE, screenplay by Karen McCullah Lutz and Kirsten Smith
- THE SECRET LIFE OF WALTER MITTY (2013), screenplay by Steve Conrad, based on the short story by James Thurber
- DALLAS BUYERS CLUB, screenplay by Craig Borten and Melisa Wallack
- GET OUT, screenplay by Jordan Peele

I also strongly urge you, if you are bitten by the screenwriting bug like I was, to follow the breadcrumbs I've left in the lists of **Further Readings** at the end of every chapter. I haven't invented the wheel here, or re-invented it. If I did anything at all it was to refine it a bit, and so if you want to check my sources, you should read these books, blogs, and articles. You'll be enhancing your knowledge and understanding of the craft if you do.

Introduction: The Process

"If you can't describe what you are doing as a process, you don't know what you are doing." ~ W. Edwards Deming

1-3-8-16-40.

What do these numbers mean? Did I spot them on a roulette wheel in Vegas? In a card game at my buddy's house? On a winning lottery ticket? Nope. These five simple numbers are the formula for structuring a screenplay, the foundation for writing a good script. How do I know this, you ask? I know this because I've spent the better part of my adult life working on understanding screenwriting, and one thing I've uncovered along the way is this simple formula—the Fibonacci sequence of screenwriting, if you will. Countless hours of self-directed search, thousands of dollars of hard-earned tuition money, endless toil and trials and tribulations led me to this basic understanding of the screenwriting process.

Okay, you say, giving me the benefit of the doubt. *Please explain further.* Happily: 1 is the one **logline** that you shall write to help you guide your story to completion like the North Star guided sailors of old. 3 is the number of **acts** you shall create from this one logline in order to lay the foundation for your scripts structure. 8 is the number of **sequences** that you shall develop from these three acts to develop your story into a feature length movie. 16 is the number of **beats** you shall write based on those eight sequences to begin to add muscle and sinew to your structural skeleton. And finally, 40 is the number of **scenes** you will create to add fleshy details to your creation so that you may then move on to writing and polishing your screenplay. Sounds simple enough, right? Simple yes. Easy? Not necessarily. It will take you time, and hard work, to reach the finish line, but this little 5-step process will help guide you from idea to finished script, I promise you.

So, where does this formula come from, you want to know? Did it spring from the head of Zeus, like Athena, goddess of wisdom? Perhaps it was always there, like gravity, and it just took a while for someone to discover it? Well, I'm not Einstein, so I can't, and won't, take credit for its discovery. What I do know is that it works.

A better question might be why did I go looking for it in the first place? Probably because like many of you reading this book, I had heard, somewhere along the way, that there existed this mythical creature, this Hollywood avatar, this Universal unicorn (pardon the puns), called *The Formula*. The secret behind every successful Hollywood blockbuster. The map to fame and riches. The Holy Grail of the Filmic Arts. If you love movies even half as much as I do, you know what I'm talking about.

I've seen this formula at work time and time again in movies from every age of Hollywood cinema from the advent of sound in the 1930s (and even before in the masterworks of Keaton and Chaplain and Griffith) right up to the special effects laden box office smashes of today, from Lubitsch to Wilder to Kubrick to Cameron and Spielberg.

Movie reviewers and critics pay respect to it and deride it, sometimes when talking about the same movie. Agents and producers swear they know it when they see it, and unless you, Young Screenwriter, know it too, they will refuse your entry into the magical kingdom of Hollywood. If you've seen more than a couple movies, and spent more than a few hours trying to figure out why all these successful films work so well, you've heard it said that it's because all these successful Oscar-winning, Box Office-smashing successes follow *The Formula*. So, you ask around, maybe even take a writing class or two, to see if you can spy out this magical elixir. But no one seems to know exactly what that formula is. They can show you examples, from CASABLANCA to ET, and they can discuss at length the merits of the films that adhere to it, but when you ask them to spell it out, in simple terms that you, the novice can understand, they look at you like you're some kind of idiot.

Well, I'm here to tell you that you're not. You just haven't been taught the process of screenwriting. And it is a process. A process that through practice and repetition can be learned, understood, and applied. Structure, or the formula, is fundamental to this process. Virtually every working writer I know will say so. It may take a little time, and more than a little hard work, but I promise you, if you're serious about it and apply yourself, and more importantly once you start seeing screenwriting as a working process, and not just as the gift of inspiration and talent, you too will come to appreciate the beauty and simplicity of it.

The next logical question is why does it matter? Why learn a formula, why pay respect to the process? Won't that just kill your "creativity"? The answer to that,

I strongly believe, is a resounding "No!". Because more important than any movie critic or reviewer, far more important than any agent or producer, *audiences* understand what makes a good screen story, and they acknowledge that with their hard-earned dollars. Even if they can't articulate how or why a film works, they can feel it working, and when it does, when the story is hitting on all cylinders, they reward the well-crafted story at the box office. This process has worked for THE WIZARD OF OZ. It worked for THE AVENGERS. It works in little movies like LEGALLY BLONDE and big movies like STAR WARS. It works in horror films, comedies, and dramas. Romances and tragedies. Indie films and Hollywood blockbusters. And it all starts with understanding the simple little formula of 1-3-8-16-40.

But why *these* numbers? Why 1-3-8-16-40? Why any numbers at all? Scripts are written in words, not mathematical equations. If there are numbers in them, they're usually spelled out, or in the title. Maybe it's because I was a rocket scientist (at NASA) before I was a student of screenwriting that I have this appreciation for math and numbers. Maybe it's because like all the great mysteries of life, underneath them lie simple concepts like $E = mc^2$, $F = mA$, and $1 + 1 = 3$ (just kidding!).

On the surface, screenwriting, like all writing, appears to be a confused jumble of words, sentences, and even shorthand. Great writing, it is said, has nothing formulaic about it. It is, per the reigning mythos, the result of capricious inspiration and fortunate genius. You can either write, or you can't, goes the oft-heard cliché. Well, I respectfully disagree. Anyone who puts in the time (and it takes time!) and effort (a whole lot of effort!) can create a well-structured script. Especially if you understand how screen stories are supposed to work. That's what this book is all about. Understanding the process, and here's the tricky part, the part that takes work, lots of work, putting it to use to create great screenplays. Practice helps you learn how to shape and mold the flesh that surrounds the skeletal structure of a script.

If you are only good at structuring, however, you've only won half the battle. An important half, but not the whole enchilada. The process of screenwriting isn't only about understanding a simple formula. It is in fact, as anyone will tell you, an art that requires not only a knowledge of structure, but also a healthy dose of "creativity". So am I hedging my bets here, you're probably wondering right about now? No, I am not. Allow me to explain. I had a great screenwriting teacher at USC named Paul Lucey. Paul had a gift for summarizing ideas about screenwriting in short, pithy phrases. One of his favorite was *new wine, old bottles*. He used this catchy mantra whenever a student would attempt to argue with him that structure kills creativity, that it is somehow antithetical to good screenwriting. For Paul, this was utter nonsense, and eventually I came to agree with him (though not without testing this truism of his over and over again). Why do so many young writers struggle with such a simple idea?

Think of it this way: when you drink the wine, you don't really notice the bottle. All you care about, if you care about wine at all, is how it hits the palette. A great wine is full of remarkable subtleties and hidden pleasures. It has a complexity that a cheap wine doesn't. And yet the cheap wine, the one that cost five bucks, comes in pretty much the same glass bottle as the Lafite Rothschild (2009) that goes for almost 20 grand a case. It's the wine inside the bottle that makes all the difference, of course, but without the bottle what do you have? A puddle of red liquid. That is the simple beauty of *new wine, old bottles*. It's the real formula for screenwriting success: one part structure and one part creativity.

So let's get started...

PART 1

Structuring
the Screenplay

Finding the Concept

Where do you find your ideas? This is one of the most common questions a working screenwriter is asked. A good idea, some folks say, writes itself. Not writers though; they know that's not true. Not even close. Ideas, no matter how good, aren't movies, they are just the kernel, the seed, from which a good movie might grow. Ideas come in all shapes and sizes, and frankly, they are a dime a dozen. In my years as a screenwriting teacher, I've rarely encountered a student who couldn't come up with an interesting idea for a movie. I have a drawer full of good ideas for scripts myself, and so will you once you start thinking about it.

You can find ideas virtually anywhere. In your own personal history (MY LIFE AS A DOG), your own daily trials and tribulations (8 MILE). You can find ideas in newspapers (SPOTLIGHT), in social media (THE SOCIAL NETWORK), in line talking to a stranger at the grocery store. The trick isn't finding ideas. It's turning that idea into a good story.

Most writers I know have an "idea file" somewhere handy. You should start keeping one, if you haven't already. Some writers jot their ideas in little notebooks they carry around with them, or type them up in a computer file, or scribble them on paper napkins they stash in an idea drawer. In fact, if you just listen, you'll hear people say to you, especially if they know you are a writer, that such-and-such or so-and-so or this-or-that would make a great movie. And you know what? They're probably right. Why? Because a great story can be developed from almost any half-way decent idea.

WHAT IF?

Another way to find ideas is to play the "what if" game—to brainstorm. The classic example of a writer playing the "what if" game is Bob Gale, who co-wrote BACK TO THE FUTURE with director Robert Zemeckis. Gale tells a story of visiting his family one summer while in college, and finding his father's high-school yearbook in the basement. Looking at the picture of his 18-year-old dad, he asked himself, *'What if I had gone to school with my dad, would I have been friends with him?'* The light bulb went off, and he had the idea for what became one of the most successful film franchises in history.

The first question you need to answer when trying to decide if an idea is a good one or bad one is, does it excite you? Does it speak to you? Move you? Make you feel genuinely passionate? Because it better. Otherwise you will not be able or willing to put in the long hours of hard work necessary to develop that idea into a full-fledged screenplay. Many a student has started working on developing their idea into a script only to realize shortly after diving into the deep end of the writing pool that they don't want to make the swim across these shark-infested waters to the glorious beach that lies on the other side of that turbulent channel. Those ideas usually end up as unfinished scripts, or in the scrap heap. There is no substitute for passion, for that burning desire to finish what you started.

But passions may and probably will cool over time. One way to keep the fires stoked is to understand the craft of screenwriting, the process of turning an idea into a story, so you can get more and more excited about your project as it grows and develops. Ask the farmer. It's the fruits of the labor, watching your hard work grow into something beautiful and delicious, that make all the necessary effort worthwhile.

FROM IDEA TO CONCEPT

Once you have an idea you are excited about, the next question you must ask is can this idea be turned into an actual premise for a movie? The best stories (and movies) seem to follow a simple premise: *Someone we care about wants something very badly and is having a very hard time getting it.* So, the first test of whether your idea will make a good movie is to see if it fits this premise. If it does, you probably have a good idea for a movie. In Hollywood, they often call this basic premise the **concept.** *Air Force One is hijacked with the President on board, and he's the only one who can foil the terrorists plot* (AIR FORCE ONE); *a seemingly indestructible humanoid cyborg is sent from the future to assassinate a waitress, whose unborn son will lead humanity in a war against the machines, while a soldier from that war is sent to protect her at all costs* (TERMINATOR).

The concept is king in Hollywood. Jeffrey Katzenberg, who ran both Disney and DreamWorks film studios, once said in a now famous memo to Disney executives: "In the dizzying world of movie making, we must not be distracted from one fundamental concept: the idea is king. If a movie begins with a great, original idea, chances are good it will be successful, even if it is executed only marginally well. However, if a film begins with a flawed idea, it will almost certainly fail, even if it is made with 'A' talent and marketed to the hilt."

Producer Robert Kosberg (TWELVE MONKEYS, COMMANDO), who's known in Hollywood as the pitch king, says this about concepts in his book *How to Sell Your Idea to Hollywood*: "Screenwriters usually focus on the craft of screenwriting—plot and developing characters. But these all fall aside if the initial concept is not clear. Find great ideas. Keep asking yourself, do you have a good idea here?"

If you have a strong enough concept, you can, with a little luck and the right connections, sell that concept even before you've written the script. If you want to sell your screenplay in Hollywood, you have to understand that the concept is everything to the decision makers who can **greenlight** a film. But if you want to have your name follow the words "Screenplay by" in the opening titles, you better know how to turn your concept into a screenplay. Otherwise someone else will be hired to finish the job for you.

MOVIES MUST MOVE

Another major consideration when evaluating ideas and turning them into concepts is understanding that movies have to move. That's why they're called "movies". They are *motion* pictures. Not paintings. Without movement, movies would just be still photography. You can write an entire novel about someone just sitting at a desk thinking about how to solve a problem for the entire story, but a movie based on that idea featuring even the most attractive actor or actress just sitting there thinking, and doing nothing at all, will bore an audience to tears. This is because you can't see a character's thoughts in movies; you can only see their actions.

A good concept requires creating a character who must *do something* to achieve their goal. Developing an active character is critical. The more challenging that something is that the character must do, the better. If their goal, what they want, is to climb a mountain, make it Mt. Everest! If it's to steal a whole lot of money, make it a bank vault as tough to break into as Ft. Knox (OCEAN'S ELEVEN).

Putting action into your movie doesn't mean you are writing an action movie. Action movies are just one **genre** of film, one type of movie, that plays on one of the inherent strengths of cinema—movement. SPEED and DIE HARD are great examples. But "character" movies like MY LEFT FOOT and WHEN HARRY MET SALLY also know that action is crucial to a good screen story.

Watch the famous "I'll have what she's having" scene in WHEN HARRY MET SALLY. It's a very simple dialogue scene with two people sitting at a table in a diner, discussing honesty in relationships. Harry is telling Sally that he lies to his sexual partners so that he doesn't have to get "romantic" with them after sex. She's of course disgusted by his boorish behavior. The dialogue is crisp and wonderful, no doubt, but watch the scene again, and notice how much action is compressed into a dialogue heavy scene. First, they are eating together. This gives the actors something to do besides yammer on and on. As the scene continues, Sally reworks her sandwich as she tells Harry how glad she is that she never got involved with him in that way. When she calls him out on his shoot and run lovemaking style, he tells her no one has ever complained to him about his "skills" in bed. She laughs, saying of course not, because they've been basically lying to him too. When he doesn't believe this could be possible, she proceeds to *act out* how a woman could fake an orgasm and he'd never know. Her *actions*, from gentle moans to wild gesticulations of ecstasy, do as much or more to prove her point in this scene as all the dialogue she speaks. In fact, the scene would be flat and a little pedantic without her actions. And not nearly as funny or memorable.

The same principle applies to every movie premise. If you don't give your characters something to do, you risk boring your audience to tears. You give your director and actors little if anything to work with to visually and emotionally craft the scenes you've written if you're not careful to develop the action in your story.

HIGH CONCEPT STORIES

Now there are some ideas that on the surface appear to be better than others. These ideas, in Hollywood parlance, are often called **high concept** ideas. These ideas, under the right circumstances, have a shot at selling themselves. The premise of a high concept story is so good that you can literally see the movie playing in your head when someone pitches the idea to you. **High concept** stories can be easily summarized, and pitched to producers and agents who can easily understand them, in a short, clearly stated premise. This short summary is sometimes called an elevator **pitch** because it can be told in the time it takes an elevator to go from the parking garage to the penthouse floor where the high muckety mucks who make the decisions about whether or not to finance a movie (often called **green-lighting** a movie) reside. A perfect example of a high concept movie is SPEED. *An LAPD cop must rescue the riders on a city bus rigged with a bomb programmed* *to explode if the bus slows down below 50 mph.* A simple, clear story, full of action you can practically see just in this one sentence description or **logline**.

These high concept stories are often contrasted with **low concept** stories which are usually more concerned with character development and other subtleties of storytelling that are not quickly or easily summarized in one sentence. Some writers make it their goal to only look for high concept stories, thinking that this is the only thing Hollywood wants, and they refuse to explore any other ideas. Many a young writer becomes hung up on the quest for the perfect high concept idea, and this can handicap individual creativity, so be careful. In the independent film world, there have been many successful low-concept stories. Here's a short list of a few good recent low concept movies:

- Bird Man
- Juno
- Little Miss Sunshine
- Lost in Translation
- Moonlight
- Room
- Spring Breakers
- Winter's Bone
- The Wrestler

These films weren't financed by major studios, though, so don't expect Hollywood to beat a path to your door if you write a low concept story. You'll likely be on your own if you want to get a film like this produced. It's no small challenge to get an indie film financed, but if the script is good enough, low concept films can be successfully made. As a novice writer, what's important is to ask yourself, can your story be summed up in a simple initial premise? *Is it a story about someone we care about, who wants something very badly and is having a very hard time getting it?*

WHAT COMES FIRST, CHARACTER OR PLOT?

As you begin to develop your idea into a concept or premise, you may find yourself asking this question: What comes first, character or plot? This question makes for a false either/or dichotomy. In fact, both come first, because you can't have a good story without both. Character and plot must be connected, and that connection has to be strong for a script to be successful. Imagine a coin with only one side. You can't. A coin always has two sides, that's what makes it a coin. So, it is with a screen story. Two sides. Character and Plot. Bound together by the glue of desire—the *want*, the *need*, for something.

It may be constructive to see where this chicken and egg argument started, and how it has developed over time. To do so, we need to briefly discuss two important characters in the evolution of the art of the story: **Aristotle**, for whom plot was paramount, and **Lajos Egri**, who illuminated Aristotle by arguing that character is more important than plot.

Aristotle was an ancient Greek philosopher; his writings covered a wide array of subjects—from physics to music, rhetoric to politics and government. Today we'd call him a renaissance man, and ironically, it's works by him and his contemporaries that helped inspire the actual Renaissance. Aristotle was also a student of the greatest philosopher, Plato, and later a teacher to Alexander the Great. These experiences, as student and teacher, provided him with an arena for testing out his ideas, one of which was his theory of storytelling.

Aristotle's seminal work on storytelling, *Poetics,* is the earliest known work on dramatic theory (at the time most drama was written as poetry). In it, Aristotle described storytelling as "imitative". For example, poetry, he said, imitates life using language; music imitates life through rhythm and harmony. Aristotle believed that imitation is natural to human beings, and constitutes one of our advantages over animals.

Aristotle went on to subdivide dramatic storytelling into **tragedy** and **comedy**, and differentiated the two by stating that comedy is a dramatic imitation of men worse than average; whereas tragedy imitates men slightly better than average. Those still may be the best definitions of the two sides of the dramatic mask ever.

Sadly, only the first book of his *Poetics*, the one on tragedy, survives. In it, Aristotle taught that tragedy is composed of six elements: plot-structure, character, style, thought, spectacle, and lyric poetry. Four of these are critical to our discussion: plot, character, style, and spectacle. The other two we will discuss in Part Two of this book. Of the first two, Aristotle stated that the characters in a drama are merely a means for driving the story; the plot, not the characters, must be the chief focus. In further defining the plot, Aristotle says this in the *Poetics*:

> *[L]et us now consider the proper construction of the... Plot, as that is at once the first and the most important thing... We have laid it down that a tragedy is an imitation of an action that is complete in itself, as a whole*

of some magnitude; for a whole may be of no magnitude to speak of. Now a whole is that which has beginning, middle, and end.

There it is, in that last sentence, the first, basic formula for all stories—a **beginning, middle,** and **end.** That, ladies and gentlemen, is your basic **plot**, and the beginning, middle, and end, those are the three **acts** of your screenplay, as we will see in Chapter Four. Plot in the movies is that basic three-part structure, nothing more and nothing less. Your story must have them to be a story, as Aristotle said, for a *whole* (story) may be of no *magnitude* without them. Character must therefore be secondary, at least according to Aristotle.

A couple thousand years after Aristotle laid out his theory of storytelling in the *Poetics*, Lajos Egri came along to argue against Aristotle's view that character was secondary to plot. Egri was the author of *The Art of Dramatic Writing*, a book about playwriting. The book though has since been used to teach not just playwriting, but the writing of short stories, novels, and, yes, screenplays. That Egri's ideas should so easily cross over different storytelling media should tell you something about the nature of storytelling (the formula or process is the same, or at least similar, regardless of the medium), as well as something about the quality of Egri's ideas (they have a universality to them that all good theories seem to possess).

Central to Egri's argument is his claim that the best stories follow a logical progression of **thesis**, **antithesis**, and **synthesis**, and do so to prove the "premise". Philosophers calls this the **dialectic** approach to structure. Notice that Egri sees story as having three parts, just as Aristotle did. He gives them different names, but the number of components he does not change. When we talk about **three act structure** later, we will use this dialectical approach as a tool to help create the three acts of your scripts.

THEME

Lajos Egri believed a **well-defined character** drives the plot themselves. But what makes a "well-defined" character? For Egri, it was **theme**. To his mind, the character drives the plot, but not as I (and many others) have proposed through want, but instead through **theme**.

A theme, or **premise**, as Egri describes it, is a thematic truth. In *The Art of Dramatic Writing*, he offers as an example of a premise: "stinginess leads to ruin." Once having settled on this theme, Egri writes, the playwright can then detect in that statement the suggestion of a story's beginning, middle, and end: first, the establishment of an obsessively stingy character; next, the collision of that character's stinginess with inevitable opposition, or antithesis; and finally, the character's ruin. Character comes first, and plot flows from character based on theme.

So, who is right? Aristotle or Egri? Well, if you look at our own initial premise for what makes a good movie, the answer should be obvious. Both character and plot are equally important. We're going to start with structure (plot) just to keep things simple, but you can just as easily start with character (and we will see how in Chapter Two). The point to remember is that *you cannot have a good movie without both a good character and a good plot*, and just as importantly, to write a good screen story, you must connect the character to the plot.

SIMPLE STORIES, COMPLEX CHARACTERS

We should mention one last thing about plot and character before we move on. Many a novice writer gets caught up in thinking that the key to a great movie is a complex story, filled with all kinds of plot twists and machinations. This could not be farther from the truth.

The examples I will cite in this book all have one thing in common. Their plots are incredibly simple, so simple you can with a little effort summarize them in one sentence (a logline!). You can certainly pitch the entire story of each, beginning, middle, and end, in less than the time it takes the elevator to go from the first to the fourth floor, let alone all the way up to the penthouse. That simplicity of story is one of the secrets to their success. The importance of a simple story cannot be overstressed.

This doesn't mean these films don't have great twists in them. They all do. A really good twist in the plot can take a good script and make it great in fact, as we will discuss in Part Two. What it does mean is that the story is simple enough for the audience to follow, which thus allows them the time they need to connect with and understand the hero of each story.

The fact is most great movies are constructed around very simple ideas, simple stories with very basic plots that if you are observant enough, or have seen enough movies, you recognize as such. Most of us don't always remember the plots of our favorite movies. It takes some genuine thought to reconstruct a movie's plot, even one we just saw the other day. Most of us, however, do remember our favorite characters. Dorothy Gale, Sam Spade, Luke Skywalker, Indiana Jones. In fact, you know you've watched a mediocre **B-movie** when you can remember the plot better than the characters that were in the film.

As a student at USC Film School back in the day, my favorite writing teacher, Paul Lucey, used to iterate this mantra over and over and over again: *simple stories, complex characters.* Most of us, even though we were smart enough, talented enough, and/or lucky enough to get into USC, either did not believe Paul at first or didn't understand what he was talking about. We didn't notice at first that there's nothing terribly complicated about the plot to THE WIZARD OF OZ, STAR WARS, or RAIDERS OF THE LOST ARK. But the characters we all loved were rich, well-rounded, characters that we connected with on a deep, fundamental level. We had to go through the process of trying to write a screenplay before we began to understand and appreciate this dictum: *simple stories, complex characters.*

EXERCISES

Exercise 1: Start an **idea file.** List 10 ideas that you think would make great movies. Use the "What If" game to help you brainstorm ideas.

Exercise 2: Which of these ideas would make for a good high concept story and which ones would make good low concept stories?

Exercise 3: Choose two of them, one high concept and one low concept, and in just two or three sentences only, describe the main character, the plot, and their goal for each concept.

FURTHER READINGS

Poetics by Aristotle

The Art of Dramatic Writing by Lajos Egri

2 Creating the Character and Plot

Why is Dorothy such a memorable heroine in THE WIZARD OF OZ? Why is Sam Spade such an unforgettable antihero in THE MALTESE FALCON? What makes each of them a great lead character? How does a writer go about creating a strong protagonist like these two movie heroes? If you look at our initial premise for what makes a good story (*someone we care about wants something very badly and is having a very hard time getting it*), you can see the answer starts with creating a character that the audience will care enough about to watch intently for a couple hours.

CHARACTER

The **character**, that person *we care about*, the person who *wants something very badly* goes by many names: **hero, protagonist**, **lead.** These all describe who the main character of your story is. This character's actions drive the story. They are the person that audiences attach themselves to, the vessel through which the story is mostly communicated. Creating a strong lead character is critical to creating a good screenplay.

A question I often hear from students as they try to develop a main character is, *does the hero have to be likeable?* What about the **antihero**? Ever since Jimmy Cagney burst on screen in THE PUBLIC ENEMY, later followed by Humphrey Bogart in a raft of great roles including Philip Marlowe in THE MALTESE FALCON, there have been numerous examples of main characters that are a little (and sometimes a lot) hard to like. Jim Carrey's character in LIAR LIAR is not a likeable guy. These antiheroes do things we often disapprove of, yet we love them anyway. How can that be? And more importantly how can that work in a screenplay?

My good friend and fellow writing instructor Sal Cardoni likes to use the word "watchable" in place of "likeable", and I think this is a good way to explain the fact that we can have heroes or antiheroes as lead characters. Most people want to be around people they like, so the likeable hero is the most obvious choice. If you, the screenwriter, want the audience to sit still for two hours and stay involved in your movie, creating a likeable protagonist makes sense.

But we all know that one guy, or gal, who despite all their flaws, all their unlikeable qualities, we enjoy hanging out with. They do the things that we, for whatever reason, are either too scared, too civilized, or just too nice to do. And we're fascinated by them. We can spend two hours with them and have a good time. You can think of the antihero as just this type of person, and properly constructed, they too can make for a great main character.

For example, Elle Woods in LEGALLY BLONDE is incredibly likeable. She's sweet, she gets along well with others, and she loves her boyfriend. She's also terrifically cute. What's not to like about a character like that? On the other hand, Ron Woodruff, the protagonist of DALLAS BUYERS CLUB, is a homophobic, drug-abusing, jackass. He isn't very likeable at all, at least early on, but in his initial self-destructiveness, he is eminently watchable. He's such a rowdy, hell-raisin', good ol' boy in fact, that we can hardly take our eyes off him.

DIMENSION

Elle and Ron have what writers call **dimension**. They are well-rounded, well-defined, believable characters. Although Elle is certainly likeable, she's also not without her flaws. She's incredibly naïve, a bit of a spoiled sorority girl, and more concerned about landing a marriage proposal than landing a great job after college. Woodruff may be a redneck, but he also seems to have a conscience, he's clearly not stupid, and he certainly appears to know how to live life to the fullest. Each exhibit what psychologist Carl Jung would call a shadow side to their dominant personality traits, and that shadow side gives these characters dimension.

ARCHETYPES

Elle and Ron are what Carl Jung would call **archetypal** characters. The term "archetype" has its origins in ancient Greek, and roughly translated means "original pattern". Jung believed that universal, mythic characters—archetypes—are models (patterns) of people and their behaviors or personalities.

Although there are many different archetypes, for our purposes two of the most helpful in developing a strong character are **persona** and **shadow**. The persona is how we present ourselves to the world. Shadow is part of the unconscious mind and is composed of repressed ideas, weaknesses, desires, instincts, and shortcomings, in other words, our inner needs or character flaws.

Elle's persona is the bubbly, naïve sorority girl. Ron's persona is the hell-raisin' cowboy. Elle's shadow is her deep insecurity about her self-worth, which is demonstrated in her need to be validated as a woman by receiving a marriage proposal from her college sweetheart Warner. Ron's shadow is his moral conscience, his need to do the right thing no matter what the cost to his cowboy image. It should be apparent that persona and shadow are in conflict with each other. This opposition helps create the kind of tension which a writer can use to develop a character, to show how they change over time. As you grow as a writer, you will want to delve more deeply into human psychology, but for right now just remember that your goal as a screenwriter is to create a well-rounded, believable lead character, a hero with dimension.

PLOT

The next part of the description of what makes a good story that we'll focus on (someone we care about who wants something very badly *and is having a very hard time getting it*) is what we call "**plot**". Plot is what Aristotle described in his *Poetics* when he laid out his theory of story structure: *[L]et us now consider the proper construction of the... Plot as... a whole... which has beginning, middle, and end.* Novelist E. M. Forster described plot as the cause-and-effect relationship between the events described in a story. *This happened, so then that happened, and the result of that was this happening.* Plot is the events in the story that lead us logically from beginning to middle to end. Plot is constructed through the order in which we as writers lay out the sequence of events (the **scenes**) that make up the story.

Going back to our original story premise, you'll notice that it's not enough for the hero to want something badly, he or she must also have a very hard time getting it. In dramatic writing, that *hard time* is defined in two important ways that connect character and plot: **want** and **need**.

OUTER GOAL

Want and need are what connect "character" (someone who wants something very badly) with "plot" (and is having a very hard time getting it). The want is the character's outward **goal**. The goal is that thing that the protagonist wants to achieve, acquire, accomplish so badly that he or she is willing to go through hell to get it. The goal will almost always be something external, physical, or tangible. In THOR, the hero wants to be king. In TOY STORY, Woody wants to be Andy's favorite toy. In THE SECRET LIFE OF WALTER MITTY, Walter wants to find the missing negative #25, the quintessence of Life.

The strongest goals seem like impossible objectives. In RAIDERS OF THE LOST ARK, Indy wants to find the Ark of the Covenant before the Nazis do. In LEGALLY BLONDE, Elle wants to win Warner back even after he dumped her and left for Harvard. The desire to get a job or win a bet isn't strong enough to sustain an entire story unless that goal feels almost unattainable to the audience. If it's not *very hard* to achieve, the reader won't care enough to remain involved with the character and the plot.

MOTIVATION

The protagonist must be motivated to succeed, so creating strong **motivation** is critical to creating a good main character. Motivation, wanting something very badly, is also what brings action to the plot. To get something you want, you must *do* something to get it. To get something you really want, more than anything in the world, you will go to any lengths, do almost anything, to get it.

What about a character who doesn't want to die, be killed, lose their head to the guillotine, you say? Not interesting enough, I say. They must want to stay alive for a reason. For love (THE ODYSSEY), for revenge (THE COUNT OF MONTE CRISTO), for the pot of gold at the end of the rainbow. These are all believable, powerful motivations for a lead character. The protagonist of your story must want something, very badly, and have a very hard time getting it.

You might pull it off in a novel or poem, but in a movie, a static main character, the opposite of an active one, will be the death of your script. Do yourself a favor and create a character who must actively work to get what they want. It will make your job as a screenwriter, which is difficult enough as it is, just a little bit easier. No matter what genre you're working in, make sure that you create a protagonist who must take action, who must be proactive, in order to get what they want. There are a few more things you will have to add to your concept to turn it into great movie, but this is where you should start. *Character. Plot. Want.* Thus, it has been, and thus it will always be in the art of dramatic writing.

STAKES

Characters who are doing something are much more watchable, and probably more likeable too, than characters who do nothing. Action, as we said in Chapter One is key to developing plot and character. Characters who are doing something *for a good reason*, who have a powerful **motivation** to accomplish their goal, are even better. And the key to creating powerful motivation in a character is to give them an overwhelming reason to accomplish their goal—in other words, to set the **stakes** so high that your character will be motivated to do almost anything to achieve their goal. High concept movies tend to have big, sometimes improbably huge, stakes, whereas low concept ones tend to have smaller, more realistic stakes.

SPEED is a classic example of setting the stakes high. In SPEED, Keanu Reeves' character wants to save the passengers on that city bus very badly because he knows what the **stakes** are if he fails. Life and death are often the stakes in movies, just for this reason. If our heroic police officer does not defuse the bomb that's set to blow up on that bus full of people, then everyone, him included, will die. If Bruce Willis can't outwit Alan Rickman in DIE HARD, Willis' wife will die. If Dorothy can't get back to Kansas, she'll never see her beloved Auntie Em again. Those are the kind of stakes a writer needs to create in order to motivate a character.

When setting the stakes high for your main character, you should also remember that "high" is a relative term. The stakes must be high *for the hero.* In the comedy THE ENGLISHMAN WHO WENT UP A HILL BUT CAME DOWN A MOUNTAIN, the town's pride is all that's at stake when the inhabitants of a small Welsh village are told that their "mountain" is only a hill by a pair of snooty English cartographers. The world isn't going to end if they can't change the cartographers' minds, the town won't disappear into a sinkhole, and no one is going to die. But within the world of the movie, losing their mountain is a really big deal for the townsfolk. Stakes are the carrot that motivates the protagonist to achieve their goal.

Setting the stakes high, or high enough, will also get the audience more emotionally involved in the story. If Bruce Willis just has to outgun Alan Rickman in DIE HARD, that's one thing, and might be fun to watch, at least for a while, and perhaps longer for a small audience of hard-core action fans. If Willis must defeat Rickman to save his wife's life, now we have engaged the audience in the protagonist's struggle. Now viewers will really care whether Willis succeeds or fails, because there's something big at stake.

Sounds simple enough then, right? Come up with a well-rounded character, give them something to do and a very compelling reason to do it. Throw in a good villain and some challenging obstacles, and you're on your way. If the protagonist knows what she needs to do, just have her do it. Solve some problems, make each one more difficult, and wham bang boom, you're done. Well, not so fast.

Why should anyone care about someone who only has to solve a few problems, jump a few hurdles, to succeed in life? We all have problems, right? We all have to overcome a few obstacles to get what we want. Big deal. Who cares? This is where the next important element in storytelling comes into play—the character's **inner need**, or what Aristotle and other early writers and theoreticians called the character's **flaw**.

INNER NEED

Now we need to return to plot for a moment, to further define both **character arc** and story arc. The main character in your story (also known as the protagonist) must have some weaknesses to be well-rounded and believable. In other words, they must be flawed. They must have an internal, psychological, emotional, or sometimes physical problem that is keeping them from achieving their outer goal, something unique to them that is blocking him or her from getting what he or she wants so badly to get. In other words, the hero must be their own worst enemy in many ways. That flaw is crucial to both the character and the plot, because in a dramatic narrative the character must overcome this flaw in order to achieve their ultimate goal.

The inner need usually isn't something physical—more often it's psychological or emotional in nature. The need describes in many ways what Egri was talking about when he proposed that it was theme that was paramount in a story. *Stinginess leads to ruin* is a theme, as Egri pointed out, and stinginess itself is the character flaw that will lead the hero to ruin, unless the hero changes. Often, as author K.M. Weiland points out, it requires nothing more than a realization by the protagonist that they indeed are flawed for them to succeed, but that realization must be hard earned.

People don't just change who they are, their nature, with a happy thought. To change they must suffer, they must struggle, they must have a very hard time getting what they want, and through that struggle they can then change and grow. This realization may not change anything about the characters external life, but it will always transform his or her perspective of themselves and the world around them, leaving the hero more capable of coping with their remaining external problems (the obstacles that are in the way of them achieving their desired goal). The ancient Greeks' favorite flaw was hubris, the sin of pride, as in the character of Oedipus. Pride is a great flaw for a character to have; a few other examples of inner need include: the need to have faith in others, to overcome jealousy or arrogance, to find courage or self-respect.

If the protagonist doesn't overcome this flaw, if they don't resolve their inner need, they will fail to achieve their goal, which just so happens to be another way to define tragedy. We don't see many genuine tragedies in the movies, for reasons that have more to do with economics than drama, but in Shakespeare's day tragedies were all the rage. HAMLET, KING LEAR, OTHELLO are all tragedies in which the protagonists failed to overcome their flaw, failed to resolve their inner need, and ultimately failed to achieve their goal. This failure to learn and grow is the real tragedy, and the true cause of the unhappy, tragic ending.

OBSTACLES

As you move through the various steps in the process of writing a screenplay, you will be developing both character and plot. One of the key elements in creating a strong plot is to show the character going through a *very hard time* in attempting to get what they want. This very hard time you create by laying out some very challenging **obstacles** in the path of your hero.

The more difficult it is for a character to do something, the better the plot will be. Say for example that your character wants to be a painter more than anything in the world, but he or she can't move his or her arms because he or she has cerebral palsy. To get what they want so badly, they must learn to paint the only way they can, with their foot. That seems an almost insurmountable obstacle, right? Sounds almost crazy to think someone could paint with their foot? Well that's the basic premise of the terrific Daniel Day Lewis film MY LEFT FOOT. If you've seen the movie, you know the story isn't that simple, but if you have such a character, someone who wants something very badly but is going to have a very hard time getting it, chances are you have a good concept for a movie.

Obstacles come in all shapes and sizes. Creating obstacles that your protagonist must overcome is crucial to developing a good story. How in the world is Keanu going to get all those innocent people off the bus without blowing it up if he has to keep the bus moving faster than 50 mph? That is a huge obstacle to his success. And what if the bomb was designed by a mad genius, a guy so smart he even blew up Keanu's friend and mentor on the bomb squad? Even better. How, and why, do these ever-increasing obstacles show up to keep the protagonist from achieving their desired goal? In terms of the plot, this is where the **villain**, the **antagonist**, becomes key to connecting plot and character.

HEROES AND VILLAINS

For these obstacles that show up regularly and get conveniently more difficult to surmount to be believable, the story needs an opposing force, an antagonist, to create the obstacles. The antagonist, who most people think of as the villain, acts to prevent our hero, the protagonist, from achieving their goal. There are four basic types of antagonistic force that can oppose the hero, often described in dramatic writing as the following: man vs. man, man vs. nature, man vs. society, and man vs. self. In the movies, the villain is usually one of the first three types, man, nature, or society.

It's difficult to create a believable, active, visual antagonist in the self, as that is too easily confused with our main character. Even in DR. JEKYLL AND MR. HYDE, we're clearly able to see the difference between the hero and villain, though the conflict is certainly one of man vs. self. There's another reason though that you don't usually see a hero as their own main villain, as we'll discuss in a moment, because the self as a force of opposition, is a special case of obstacle that deals with our hero's flaw or inner need.

For this opposing force to work dramatically, it must appear to be even more powerful than the protagonist. It must seem to the audience that there's no way the hero can possibly defeat the villain. In SPEED, the antagonist is Howard Payne (played by Dennis Hopper). Payne (great name for a villain, eh?) isn't just any old bad guy, he's a sociopathic master bomb builder.

In THE WIZARD OF OZ, we have an even greater villain, the scary old Wicked Witch of the West, righteously motivated by the death of her sister who is crushed when Dorothy's tornado-blown house lands right on top of her, and who will do whatever it takes including unleashing flying monkeys and killing all her new-found friends to exact her vengeance upon the young, vulnerable Dorothy, before poor Dorothy can escape her evil clutches and return to her home in Kansas.

CONFLICT

This direct opposition between hero and villain, protagonist and antagonist, we call **conflict**. And conflict is the rocket fuel that writers need to continually feed the fires of rising action, of story arc and character arc, and build them up through ever more challenging obstacles until they reach the **climax**, that fiery moment when the hero and the villain face off in direct confrontation to see who will finally get what they want, and who won't.

RISING ACTION

Obstacles should get more and more difficult to overcome as the plot develops. This ever-increasing difficulty of the obstacles, we call the **rising action**. The increasing difficulty of the challenges leads to rising actions on the hero's part to overcome the obstacles, and this is how his or her quest to achieve the goal begins to turn into a plot—a plot, most importantly, with a **story arc** built on ever greater challenges. The obstacles that lead to the rising action ultimately will lead to a **climax**—the final confrontation between hero and villain. And this climax will bring a **resolution**, a sense of completion, to the story. This resolution can be either a happy or a sad ending, and it should give the audience a sense of **closure**, though sometimes an ending is ambiguous, falling somewhere in between happy and sad. Sometimes the ending is left unresolved, leaving open to interpretation what happens to the hero. In every case however, the hero must overcome a series of obstacles in their attempt to achieve their goal.

ALLIES AND HENCHMEN

In THE WIZARD OF OZ, Dorothy's first obstacle to getting home is to navigate the Yellow Brick Road. Nothing terribly difficult there, right? Just follow that road—it is yellow and easy to see, so that shouldn't be too hard, right? One of the obstacles to achieving this simple goal though is that she's a stranger in a strange land (who accidentally killed the villain's sister upon arriving on the wrong end of a tornado in Oz), so to successfully follow even this rather simple road, she needs some friends. So, what does she do? She sets about acquiring some friends, and each one is a little more difficult to get than the last.

One way to allow the obstacles to get ever more challenging, to allow the conflict between hero and villain to build, and to hold off the final climactic moment of confrontation between hero and villain until the last possible moment, is to introduce **allies** and **henchmen** to the story. Allies are just what they sound like—friends, cohorts, companions who are recruited by the hero to help them achieve their goal.

Not all stories have them, and some have more than others (THE LORD OF THE RINGS, THE DIRTY DOZEN), but allies can be very useful, as illustrated by THE WIZARD OF OZ. The Lion, the Tinman, and the Scarecrow, all join Dorothy's quest, and they do so for not just reasons of plot, but also reasons of character. Each of them has a gripe with the Wicked Witch, so each is motivated to help Dorothy, but each also represents something about who Dorothy is, and particularly what her inner need is. Courage, Heart, and Intelligence, all of which Dorothy will require to defeat the Witch (plot). Each of them represents a small aspect of home as well as they are each played by the same actors who work on the farm in Kansas which Dorothy calls home, and which she learns to value above all other things (character).

Similarly, henchmen often represent or stand in for the villain. SPEED has virtually no henchmen, unless you included the unwitting guy who shoots the bus driver early in the chase. Other movies have multiple henchmen. A good example is the various scoundrels Alan Rickman's character Hans Gruber has assembled in DIE HARD to help him achieve his goal of ransoming the Nakatomi Plaza headquarters, ostensibly to teach the Nakatomi corporation a lesson in greed and avarice. Gruber and his heavily armed team seize the tower and take everyone inside as hostages during a Christmas party, except for Detective John McClane's estranged wife, Holly, who manages to slip away. These henchmen are smart, ruthless, muscle-bound, and well-armed killers each of whom McClane must do battle with and subdue before finally confronting Gruber directly and ultimately reconciling with his wife (plot). These henchmen, along with Gruber, also help illustrate McClane's character flaw. McClane is a cocky cowboy, a cop who has sacrificed the love of his wife and family all in the name of duty, honor, and glory. Gruber, likewise is willing to sacrifice the lives of everyone in Nakatomi headquarters to make his point. It's only when McClane surrenders his cowboy persona and his machine gun to save his wife that he shows that he's learned the most difficult lesson of all, at least for him, and thus is worthy of defeating Gruber.

LESSONS LEARNED

Another way to look at a character's flaw, or inner need, is to view it in the form of a lesson that must be learned. In THE WIZARD OF OZ, Dorothy must learn the real value of home. Unless she learns to truly value home, she will never find the courage to defeat the Wicked Witch. The villain and their henchmen, along with the obstacles they help create, function to teach the character the lesson they must learn. They continually challenge the lead character to confront their inner need, their flaw, in order to not only get what they want, to achieve their goal, but also to make the audience feel like they *earned* it.

In LEGALLY BLONDE, Reese Witherspoon's character must learn that she cannot allow men to define success for her as a woman. Her inner need, her flaw, is that she cannot feel good about herself unless she is validated by a man (whether it be her boyfriend, or her law professor). Until she learns that lesson, she will never be happy, which is all she really wanted in the first place. Once she does learn it, her goal, to live happily ever after, can be achieved. Each obstacle in her story arc is another opportunity for her to learn this lesson. The obstacles get tougher, too, which leads to what is often called a character's arc.

CHANGE/GROWTH

How are the lessons a character needs to learn about themselves developed? Lajos Egri, in his theoretical work, emphasized what he saw as the crucial role of change in all forms of life; change forces people to evolve and synthesize new philosophies in the face of one overwhelming obstacle after another in order to deal with life. Life happens, so to speak, and it happens, at least in dramatic writing, for a reason—to teach us the lessons we need to learn through confronting and overcoming our character flaws so we may grow as human beings.

Look no farther than Elle (played by Reese Witherspoon), the lead character in LEGALLY BLONDE. She is the archetypal dramatic character. She has a strong want, and an even stronger need, and she struggles mightily to resolve both before her story is finished. Most significantly, in terms of blending character with plot, she has a very strong outer goal and believable, relatable flaws (a strong inner need) which she eventually overcomes through ever increasing conflict with the antagonist (and their henchmen), ultimately learning her lesson and then finally achieving her goal.

That is how plot and character come together to tell a great story. The two work in concert, and the conflict between protagonist and antagonist is the key. Like the story arc, a **character arc** ultimately leads to a climactic moment and a resolution of the inner need or flaw, in other words to a change in character. It is in that climactic moment in the character arc that the audience must see, and more importantly feel, that the hero has finally learned their lesson, resolved their inner need. Then and only then will the audience believe the hero can defeat the villain, overcome the antagonistic force, and achieve their goal, which is to get what they so badly wanted all along.

Dorothy must learn how vitally important home really is and what it really means to her, before she can find the courage to confront and defeat the Wicked Witch. It is only through learning that lesson, a lesson painfully learned through overcoming all obstacles and finally in direct confrontation with the antagonist, that a story can reach its justifiable ending. If a writer manages to do this, they will leave their audience satisfied in the outcome of the story. By connecting the resolution of the main character's inner need (the resolution of the character arc) to the achievement of their outer goal (resolution of the story arc), screenwriters can create great screenplays.

EXERCISES

Exercise 1: Using the following movies...

- *Casablanca*
- *Silence of the Lambs*
- *When Harry Met Sally*
- *40-Year-Old Virgin*
- *Locke*
- *Get Out*

    . . . answer the following questions about each movie:

a. Who is the main character (protagonist) in each of these films?
b. Who is the villain (antagonist)?
c. What is the main character's outer goal (their want) in each film?
d. What is the main character's flaw (their inner need) in each film?

    e. What lesson does the main character need to learn in each film before they can achieve their goal?

    f. Describe the protagonist's character arc. How do they change from the beginning to the end of the story?

Exercise 2: Using one of the ideas you came up with in Chapter One answer the following:

- What does this character want (what is their OUTER GOAL)?
- What aspect of this character needs to change (what is their INNER NEED or FLAW) before they can get what they want?

Exercise 3: Then briefly describe this character's physical appearance *(gender, age, body type, hair, eyes, facial features, dress, posture, movements, mannerisms, speech, first impression):*

Exercise 4: Describe their background, which may influence their actions/ motivations. *(education, religion, family, early childhood experiences, financial situation, profession, marital status, other relationships, habits, surroundings/ environment, health:*

Exercise 5: What kind of personality do they have? *(Distinctive traits, self-image, yearnings/dreams, fears/apprehensions, sense of humor, code of ethics, attitude—optimistic? overly sensitive?):*

Exercise 6: Now write a one-page inner monologue for your hero in which the character talks about what they want and why they want it.

Exercise 7: Make a list of your favorite movie characters, then divide them into heroes and anti-heroes, or likeable and watchable protagonists.

FURTHER READINGS

The Hero with a Thousand Faces by Joseph Campbell
The Hero's Journey by Chris Vogler.

Writing the Logline

We've spent a little time discussing how plot and character must work hand in hand to create a story. In the rest of Part One, we will focus on how to structure a strong plot, and in Part Two we'll focus on creating strong characters. But you should always remember that character and plot cannot and should not be entirely separate creations. In the back of your mind, you must always be thinking about how the two connect.

To simplify the task a bit, let's begin with the process of structuring a plot for your screenplay. How do you begin? What do you need to do first to construct a simple story around which you can build a great character? The answer: start by creating the **logline**. A logline is a one (sometimes two) sentence description of the basic story. Chris Lockhart (author of the blog *The Inside Pitch*) says that a logline "conveys the dramatic story of a screenplay in the most abbreviated manner possible. It presents the major through line of the dramatic narrative without character intricacies and sub-plots. It is the story boiled down to its base." As simple as this notion might sound, it can be a real challenge for a writer to condense a story into a logline.

A well-crafted logline should do all the following:

- Tell us who the story is about (protagonist)
- ...what they are striving for (goal)
- ...and what stands in their way (antagonistic force).

If this sounds familiar, it should. The logline is basically our initial premise for what makes a good story (*someone we care about wants something very badly and is having a very hard time getting it*) specifically tailored to the idea and concept for your movie. To begin the process of creating the logline, you need to start with that definition of a good premise. Notice again the important elements of the premise:

- Someone we care about (either likeable or watchable)
- Who wants something very badly
- And is having a hard time getting it

You can start with any one of these elements: by thinking about what the goal is (*what* the hero *wants very badly*) or who the main character of your story is (that flawed protagonist that *we care about*). You can even start by thinking about the villain (the antagonistic force that is making it *so hard* for your hero to get what they so badly want).

The writer of SPEED may have come up with the villain and the booby-trapped bus full of passengers first. Then he would have built his main character, Jack Traven, around this notion. L. Frank Baum, who wrote the book that the movie THE WIZARD OF OZ is based on, may have first thought of a young, naïve, frustrated girl who wanted to escape her dreary life on a Kansas farm before he came up with the Wicked Witch and the Land of Oz. It's the classic chicken and egg conundrum, but in this case, the answer of which comes first, character, goal, or antagonist doesn't matter as much as getting started. Because another thing you will learn quickly about loglines is that writers are constantly revising them, working on them, polishing them. You will do the same thing with your logline until you have developed one that is strong enough and succinct enough to encapsulate your entire movie in a single, powerful sentence or two.

In the movie business, the logline serves several functions. One of its functions is that writers use it to quickly pitch scripts to prospective agents and producers, who are often far too busy to read an entire script. The logline is the hook that helps the writer catch a prospective agent's or producer's interest. It's a commonly held notion amongst screenwriters that agents and producers know nothing about good writing. A notion undoubtedly born of the frustration of trying to sell your script in a market filled with hundreds, if not thousands of script hawkers. If these guys knew *anything*, the thinking goes, they'd see that your script is brilliant. And they'd buy it.

Well, I hate to burst that bubble, but making movies is the business of agents and producers. It is their livelihood. If they knew nothing about good writing, they'd be out of business pretty quickly. Now they may not all be Darryl O. Selznick or Jerry Bruckheimer, but producers and agents know a good story when they hear one. They know it because they've heard thousands of them, pitched to them by writers, and they know which ones worked and which ones flopped at the box office. They know that if a writer has been able to distill their script into one very good logline, chances are good that they may have also written a good screenplay, one worth spending their very precious time reading.

The logline is also often the basis for the way a film is marketed to an audience. In the old days, you could open your TV Guide and read one-sentence summaries of all the movies and shows on television that day. Nowadays, you hit the info button on your remote control and up pops a very short description of the show you're watching. Be careful though, not to confuse logline with **tagline**. A tagline is the catchy little three- or four-word phrase you find on the movie poster, often just below the title. For example, the tagline for ARMAGEDDON was "Earth. It was fun while it lasted." Catchy, clever, but not the crystallization of the story into one powerful sentence—not a logline.

Chances are if you have the writer's calling you will already have the kernel of the logline bouncing around in your brain, needling you; it started with that idea or concept you were obsessing about. The logline takes this idea, this premise of yours, a step further by filling in the details and thus breathing life into it. So, let's write a logline then, shall we? The first step is to answer the three basic questions that will help us go from idea or concept to logline:

- Who is your movie about?
- What is it that this character wants very badly?
- Why is it so hard for them to get it?

Here's my answers: *My movie is about a mother who wants to cure her son's illness, but has no idea how to do that because she's not a doctor.* That's a start, but despite the drama of a mother with a sick child it feels a little flat, and really kind of boring if I'm brutally honest with myself (and you should be your toughest critic if you really want to become a good writer). Clearly this **first draft** needs some work before it can become a strong logline.

Let's work on developing the answer to the third question first to make it stronger: why is it so hard for this mother to cure her son? Can't she just take him to the doctor and get him a shot of penicillin? No. That would be way too easy. Not nearly challenging enough. Not very hard at all to achieve this goal. So how do we make it more difficult for this mother of ours to succeed? Well, how about if we give her son an incurable disease. Something rare and mysterious. Unless we are an epidemiologist, we will need to do some research on this subject to find the right disease for our story.

Research, it should be noted, is most definitely part of the writing process. Although there is some truth to the *write what you know* philosophy of writing, in Hollywood, writing what you have spent some time learning about is a very common, tried-and-true method of developing a good story. Many writers do quite a bit of research when they are developing a story, in fact. So, we do our research, on the internet, at the library, talking to real doctors, and lo and behold we stumble upon a disease that strikes us as potentially very good for our story: adrenoleukodystrophy. It's good because it's rare, mysterious, and sounds scary. It's a disease linked to problems with the X chromosome which causes damage to the nerves, resulting in seizures, hyperactivity, loss of speech and motor skills, and ultimately results in death within two years. Yikes!

A mother whose child has such a disease would be *desperate* to save her son. Okay, we're making progress. But why not just have mom take her kid to the Mayo Clinic and let the super-smart doctors there cure him? Because that would be too easy. The thing that makes curing her son so difficult is that this disease has *no cure*. And not only that, it's so rare, that *no one is even looking* for a cure for it. Now we're cooking with gas. These circumstances make getting what our mother wants (her son cured) very difficult to achieve indeed.

This brings us to an important concept with respect to the logline: the **stakes**. As we mentioned in Chapter Two, in a good screenplay, or any good story for that matter, something big, important, vital (sometimes even life and death itself) should be at stake for the protagonist if they fail to achieve their goal, if they fail to get what they want so badly. If there's nothing, or very little, at stake for them in the outcome, the audience may not care what happens. Because, why should they? There's no consequences to our hero's failure. In our case, however, we have this in spades. If this mother doesn't find a way to cure her son of this unpronounceable disease, he will be dead within two years. If we want to raise the stakes even higher, we could make this boy her only child, and even higher still, make it so that she cannot have any more children herself. Now losing her son would be a truly devastating blow. And from a writing standpoint, it gives our character something else that we discussed in Chapter Two that is also vitally important: the **motivation** to succeed. Remember that giving your hero a powerful reason to achieve what they are after helps you both build the plot and keep the audience interested in the outcome.

Now let's work on the character of the mother for a bit. It's not enough to just answer the question, *who is your movie about?* You must make this person someone the audience will care about. Someone they'll want to watch struggle for two hours. For dramatic purposes, to help in constructing the plot and to developing a well-rounded and believable protagonist, this character needs to be flawed in some way. She needs to have an inner need that must get resolved, otherwise we're not going to feel that she has learned anything in her journey. A character without an inner need won't have an arc.

What could be this mother's flaw? What inner need would she have to resolve before she can save her son? There are a myriad of possibilities. Remember now, that this flaw, this need, should be something internal to your main character's psychology, her inner world. She could live in Afghanistan, where women aren't allowed to walk around without a burka, let alone challenge the established medical order to find a cure for her son. But that is not a flaw, that is an unfortunate situation. She could be uneducated, not even know how to read, which would make it nigh impossible for her to do the research she'll have to do to find a cure. But again, this isn't an inner need, it's an outer circumstance. She could be an alcoholic, or obsessive compulsive. These are flaws too, no doubt, but are they the right flaw for this story?

Ideally the flaw, that inner need of the main character, should reflect somehow on the character's outer goal. In the classic film CASABLANCA, the main character, Rick, is selfish. He only thinks about himself, and saving his own skin. But when the story gets rolling, we see that his outer goal is to save his former girlfriend Ilsa, the woman that broke his heart, and her self-sacrificing, noble husband Viktor from a bunch of ruthless Nazi henchmen. This inner flaw is darn near perfect, because until Rick learns to get past his selfishness, he will never be able to save Ilsa. She and Viktor will be captured by the Nazis and executed, and the war will go on.

In THE WIZARD OF OZ, you have a naïve young girl who thinks happiness can only be found somewhere over the rainbow. She feels stuck at home on a farm in grim, black and white, Kansas. She's angry and bitter and all she can think about is her own happiness. Then a nasty old tornado blows her to the exact place she wants to be, and she quickly finds out that somewhere over the rainbow is not such a wonderful place after all. It's ruled by an evil witch, who now wants to kill her. Dorothy is painfully but believably naïve. She mistakenly believes the secret to finding happiness lies outside herself, and she'll have to learn the painful lesson that it most definitely does not. She must learn that the Wizard who promises happily ever after is a sham, and life is a struggle she needs to meet head on if she wants to stay alive and return home safely.

Naïve and selfish may sound like simple flaws, and that's because they are. So is not being confident in your own abilities to succeed (Elle in LEGALLY BLONDE), or being too much of a reckless cowboy (John McClain in DIE HARD). According to novelist Terri Dawn Smith, there are three basic character arcs for this inner journey:

- **To risk being who you really are.** The hero learns to stand up for who he is regardless of what others think.
- **To risk doing what is right.** The hero does the honest thing despite the consequences.
- **To risk connecting with others.** The hero opens up to relationships even if they bring trouble and sorrow.

This may oversimplify things a bit too much, but there's a reason all these flaws are so simple, and that's because simple flaws are very easy for the audience to understand and relate to. We've all been selfish at one time or another, we've all been too by the book, or too reckless, or too naïve, or afraid to connect with someone. And we all had to learn, often the hard way, to overcome these flaws in our character.

Now back to our mother and her dying son. What's mom's problem? Well, maybe it's as simple as she doesn't trust people, and thus she thinks that only she can save her son. She's afraid to trust anyone with her son's life. He's her only child after all, and putting his life in the hands of someone else just is not an option in her mind. This is of course a serious problem. For one, she's not a doctor and knows nothing about medicine, let alone rare autoimmune diseases. Secondly, to learn what she would need to learn to cure her son would take her years upon years, and she doesn't have that kind of time. Until she realizes that she cannot do this alone, that she must put some trust in other people, put her faith in someone else, someone like a doctor who has her son's best interests at heart but who also understands how to take what our mother has figured out on her own about this disease and turn it into a cure, only then will she be able to find a cure for her son's disease. This sounds like the perfect flaw for our main character.

Now that we have developed answers for the three basic logline questions let's take a first crack at writing a logline for this story: *A fearful mother is forced to join forces with a medical researcher she does not fully trust in order to find a cure for her only son's rare and deadly autoimmune disease.* Not bad at all. This is starting to sound like a good logline. And if it rings a bell, it should. This is, with a few gentle modifications, the basic logline for George Miller's terrific film, LORENZO'S OIL, starring Susan Sarandon and Nick Nolte. For those of you that know this film, you're probably ready to jump me in a dark hallway, because you know this is a true story movie! Not so fast I say, dodging your angry swipes and slashes. Yes, this movie is *based* on a true story, but it's also a script that was constructed around a simple story and complex characters. Whether it's based on real events, like LORENZO'S OIL, or on the wild imaginings of a fanciful writer like THE WIZARD OF OZ, the fact remains that good stories are simple ones, and simple stories can be summarized in one well-written sentence which screenwriters call a logline.

Like writing a good *haiku*, writing good loglines takes practice. The more you practice writing loglines the better you will get at creating good simple stories. Despite its apparent simplicity, however, the logline is often one of the more difficult writing concepts to learn, and to implement well. That's because most new writers haven't yet learned the *simple stories, complex characters* lesson yet. Below are a couple examples of loglines:

The Wizard of Oz—A naive Kansas farm girl transported by a terrifying tornado to a magical land must evade the evil witch now hunting her as she embarks on a dangerous journey to find the mysterious wizard who has the power to send her back home.

99 Homes—A desperate, unemployed construction worker chooses to go to work for an unscrupulous realtor in order to save his family home from foreclosure.

The beauty of constructing a logline first, before you start writing your script, is that creating this one-sentence summation of your movie will force you to keep the story as simple as possible. If you don't keep it simple, you'll quickly find that you can't summarize your movie in one-sentence. This of course can be incredibly frustrating at first, because many a novice writer thinks that their story is great because it's so complex, full of wild and crazy twists and turns, and fascinating tangents. But when they attempt to pitch a story like that to an agent or producer, they quickly find themselves lost in the explanation, and if they are paying attention to their audience, that they are boring them to tears.

You should not rush this step in the process, either. Starting here with the logline is vital, but so is putting the time in to getting the logline right. If the logline doesn't work, if it's broken or faulty, the script you are going to go on and write is almost surely not going to work either. This may be the most important reason to write a logline first, and to spend the time to make it as good as you possibly can. It takes most writers weeks and usually months to write a script. If you start off with a faulty premise, a logline that doesn't work well, you will end up wasting a lot of precious time working on a script that is inherently flawed.

That's why the dirty little secret of many a writer, even the best, is that they often go back to the logline after they've started writing to tweak it, modify it, or sharpen it, once they've begun to see the problems in their story's structure (structural issues that we will address in depth in the following chapters). This highlights another very important reason that a logline can be an incredibly valuable tool for a writer, especially a novice writer. The logline serves as a kind of compass point, the destination on a triptych that a clever writer uses so they don't get lost on their journey from idea to finished story.

And you will be surprised, perhaps even shocked, at how often early on in your writing career you will get yourself lost. It's not unusual, and you shouldn't let it get you down. It's part of the process of learning how to write screenplays. Think about it. If you, the intrepid traveler, don't know where you're going, or how you're going to get there, you can and almost inevitably will end up somewhere you didn't want to be. Occasionally, this wrong turn may take you serendipitously to a good place. Such happy accidents are not to be ignored, but more often than not, you will not end up in a happy place. You will end up miserable, frustrated, confused, and angry. You'll want to throw your script in the trash, and start all over again with a new story. You will have wasted a lot of time and energy chasing imaginary rabbits down the wrong rabbit holes. You'll end up stuck in a swamp, hip deep in quicksand, or at a dead end in the road because you didn't follow the map you created for your journey. The best way to avoid this personal agony is to give yourself a direction and a destination, and in the land of screenwriting, that is done with the logline.

There's one additional reason that the logline can be a valuable tool for the screenwriter. If you're like most writers, you have friends who are writers, or friends who you tell your stories to. These friends are your sounding boards, your test subjects, the people you inflict your great movie ideas upon to get a quick reaction, a bit of encouraging feedback, to let you know if you are on the right path to screenwriting stardom. Make sure you're getting honest feedback from these fellow storytellers, and not just pats on the back and attaboys.

If you want to be collecting your award for writing prowess you will have to please an audience somewhere along the line, and a great place to start is by pitching friends, family, or fellow writers your story ideas. In a way that makes them get as excited as you are about this amazing movie you are about to write. The easiest and best way to do that is by telling them the logline of your script. If their ears perk up, if they smile and laugh, if their jaw hits the floor, mouth agape at the terror or surprise you have just created in them, you are on to something.

EXAMPLES OF LOGLINES

APOCALYPSE NOW: During the Vietnam War, Captain Willard is sent on a dangerous mission into Cambodia to assassinate a renegade American colonel who has set himself up as a god among a local tribe.

BRIDGES OF MADISON COUNTY: An Iowa housewife, stuck in her routine, must choose between true romance and the needs of her family when a handsome photographer shows up in town.

DJANGO UNCHAINED: With the help of a German bounty hunter, a freed slave sets out to rescue his wife from a brutal Mississippi plantation owner.

THE HANGOVER: Three groomsmen on a bachelor party weekend in Vegas lose their about-to-be-wed buddy during their drunken misadventures, then must retrace their steps in order to find him and bring him home for his wedding.

RESIDENT EVIL: Survivors of a science experiment gone terribly wrong find themselves trapped in a subterranean laboratory fighting off the living dead in order to stay alive.

A SCANNER DARKLY: An undercover cop addicted to a drug that creates an alternate personality struggles to capture the drug dealer—who is his alter ego.

TROPIC THUNDER: A group of spoiled actors filming a war movie in Southeast Asia suddenly find themselves in the middle of real combat.

TRAINING DAY: An idealistic rookie trains for the narcotics division with a rogue cop (in trouble with the Russian mob) and learns the hard way how to navigate the tough streets of Los Angeles.

UP IN THE AIR: A coolly detached executive who specializes in firing other people faces a crisis of conscience while training his young replacement.

THE VOW: A whirlwind romance and marriage is tragically altered after a car accident results in the bride losing all memory of her new husband, who struggles to win her heart all over again.

PRACTICE MAKES PERFECT

Practice is the best way, the only way, to hone your logline writing skills. There are several templates out there available to assist writers in constructing loglines, and the exercise below uses one, but you should remember that adhering too closely to one of these templates may leave your logline sounding rather formulaic or cliché as opposed to dramatic and intriguing. Remember that adage *new wine in old bottles* when creating your logline, and try and inject something new or fresh into your creation, while still remembering that you must convey some basic information (character, goal, etc.) so that people understand what story it is you're trying to tell. With that caveat in mind, the following is a fun simple exercise for practicing writing loglines.

EXERCISES

Exercise 1: Take one word or phrase from each column and construct three different loglines for movies.

Chapter 3 Writing the Logline **37**

Pick	Column 1	Column 2		Column 3	Column 4		Column 5	Column 6
one	_adjective(s) that describe hero's flaw_	_noun that describes who the hero is_		_action verb_	_the antagonistic force_		_action verbs_	_the hero's goal_
A	alcoholic	astronaut	must	find	gravity	in order to	find	true love
An	bitter	baker	is forced to	kill	a serial killer		kill	a lost relic
	childish	chiropractor	chooses to	escape	cancer		escape	marriage
	duplicitous	dog walker		join	the government		survive	promotion
	egotistical	extraterrestrial		defeat	his/her best friend		steal	a teddy bear
	fanatical	firefighter		save	a diabolical genius		save	his/her child
	grumpy	gambler		overcome	a bad memory		overcome	a golden fleece
	homophobic	hockey player		capture	the mafia		capture	a super model
	idealistic	married couple		outwit	a selfish banker		outwit	a cure
	jealous	SWAT team		confront	a mysterious stranger		win	a buried treasure

Example: An alcoholic extraterrestrial is forced to join the mafia in order to save a super model.

Exercise 2: Reverse engineer a logline for a recent movie you've seen.

1. Describe a recent film you've seen in a few brief sentences.

   - Who is the story about (the hero/protagonist)?
   - What is their flaw (inner need)?
   - What are they striving to achieve (the goal)?
   - What stands in their way (the villain/antagonistic force)?
   - What is at stake if they fail (what does the protagonist stand to gain or lose)?

2. Now write a logline for this film.

Exercise 3: From the 10 ideas you brainstormed for movies in Chapter 1

1. Pick two or three of these ideas and answer the following questions:

   - Who is the story about (the hero/protagonist)?
   - What is the protagonist's inner need (character flaw)?
   - What are they striving to achieve (the goal)?
   - Who or what stands in their way (the villain/antagonistic force)?
   - What is at stake for the protagonist?

2. Now write a logline for each.

FURTHER READINGS

Finding the Core of Your Story by Jordan Smith;

The Inside Pitch by Chris Lockhart at http://twoadverbs.blogspot.com/

Developing 3 Acts

Once you've written your logline, the next step in the process is to take that one-sentence summary of your story and break it up into three acts. **Breaking a story** is a very common phrase used in film and TV writing. It is the first step in giving your story idea a form—a structure. That structure starts with creating **acts**—you are breaking up your story, dividing it if you like, into more specific, and more manageable parts. Sometimes called dramatic structure, because it describes the dramatic arc of a story, this three-act structure is not something invented by the movies.

The term *act* comes from the world of the theater, where many of the writing conventions of cinema have been derived. An "act" in the theater (and in film and television) is the broadest structural unit of a story. Because plays are actual performances staged before a live audience, we "see" the "breaks" more clearly when there is a change of set, costume, or cast on stage. The act breaks in television are also more visible than the breaks in movies because we see commercials pop up, at least on commercial television. The average viewer doesn't normally notice an **act break** in a movie, but once you learn about them and try to apply them as a screenwriter they can easily be detected in virtually any movie you watch.

The real purpose of act breaks is not to let the actors change wardrobe, or to let a network sell advertising, it's to help give writers a structure, a form, that can and does help audiences better understand the tale he or she is telling. Every movie is in some ways unique, or should be, and to help audiences understand these uniquely individual works, a familiar form can be very useful. It's the *new wine in old bottles* idea once again. Though several different theories regarding act structure have been argued over the centuries, the three-act structure is the most popular. In large measure, this is because Hollywood quickly discovered, as far back as the 1910s with D.W. Griffith and THE BIRTH OF A NATION (which many scholars also see as the birth of cinematic narrative form), that this structure helps create successful, commercial movies that audiences will flock to see. In short, three act stories are the most popular. So, if you want to sell your screenplay to Hollywood, it behooves you to give it to them in a form that they understand. So, how does a writer do this? Where do you start?

First, you begin with the one simple sentence that describes your plot (and main character and their goal), your logline, and then you develop it into to three sections that describe the overall structure of your plot, in its simplest most basic terms: *beginning, middle,* and *end.* This is the same structure delineated by Aristotle in his *Poetics* all those centuries ago.

Each act in a three-act structure serves a very specific story purpose, and as we move on in the following chapters we will delve into these in greater depth, but for now, keeping with our *simple stories* mantra, we can define this form in very simple language: Act One describes the beginning of your story, Act Two describes the middle of the story, and Act Three describes the ending. More specifically we can define these acts in the following way:

ACT ONE

In this act, the protagonist (our hero) and the world he or she inhabits are set up for the audience (this is often referred to as **exposition** or the **status quo**). Somewhere, usually around the middle of the act, something occurs that knocks our unsuspecting hero off balance (not usually literally, but much more often emotionally or psychologically). This **inciting incident** (sometimes referred to as the **catalyst** or **point of attack**) sets the main events of the story in motion. At this point, our hero is forced to make a choice to deal with the changing world and take the active step of pursuing a goal related to that changed world somehow. They almost always make this choice reluctantly (we'll discuss why in later chapters), but they must decide to take action here. They must choose to leave the world of Act One for Act Two.

ACT TWO

At this point, the main character enters a new world, sometimes literally but sometimes only figuratively. This is a place they are very unfamiliar with, and one they don't know how to navigate, which makes it more difficult for them to achieve their goal. Each attempt they make to get what they want is also met with ever increasing resistance, usually because the antagonist does not want our hero to succeed (this active resistance is called **conflict** or **confrontation**). The ever-increasing difficulties are known as **complications** or **the rising action**. Ultimately, after repeated failures, each one should be more spectacular than the last, the main character reaches his or her lowest point, emotionally and/ or physically. They have just about given up hope of ever achieving their goal, of getting what they want. It seems to them, and just as importantly to the audience, that there is no way they can possibly succeed.

ACT THREE

Herein our protagonist musters up one last effort, putting everything they've learned up to this point into action and meets the antagonist head on in one final showdown. (Remember the hero began this journey with a flaw, an inner need, about which they had to learn a lesson so they could resolve that need, that flaw, if they ever hoped to succeed). The **climax**, the final showdown, occurs, the villain is defeated, and our hero finally gets what they've been wanting all along (and sometimes, as in a tragedy, doesn't). Then comes the **resolution**, where equilibrium returns, but importantly not an exact restoration of the original status quo. This new equilibrium, sometimes called the **denouement**, should reflect how our hero has changed and grown since we first met them. At this point, the **dramatic question** (will our hero get what they want or not?) has been resolved, and the audience can leave the theater and go home satisfied.

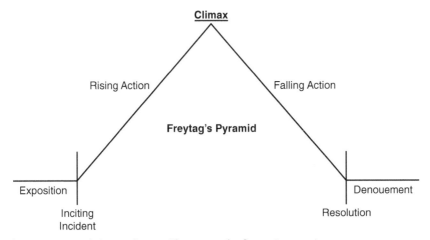

Figure 1 Freytag's inverted pyramid structure for dramatic narrative.

Screenplay guru Syd Field was one of the first folks to point out the validity of this structure to cinema. His book *Screenplay,* written in 1979, was a bible for many a novice writer when I was in college. Field was a major proponent of structure as the foundation for all screenwriting. Field's work was based in part on Aristotle's *Poetics,* but also on Gustav Freytag's *Dramatic Techniques* from which he borrowed the classic inverted pyramid in *Figure 1* above to illustrate dramatic narrative structure. Field also drew on his experiences both as a writer and an instructor to codify what he believed to be the fundamentals of screenplay structure.

In classical three act structure, a writer first sets up the story's main character and their world (often called the **set up**). In screenwriting, Field said this should be done within the first twenty to thirty pages of the script (Act One). Then the protagonist makes a choice to actively attempt to achieve a goal that turns the story in a new direction, thus beginning Act Two. This second act focuses on the protagonist's ever-increasing struggle to achieve their goal, which Field called the **confrontation** and Freytag the **rising action**. Act Three depicts the protagonist's final attempt to achieve his or her goal, whether successful or not, as well as the aftermath, which Field called the **resolution** and **denouement**.

BEGINNING, MIDDLE, END

We will more closely examine some of the elements that Field and Freytag stressed as important to dramatic structure, like the **inciting incident** and **midpoint,** in later chapters, but for now let's start by focusing on the simple. That is let's start with the basic plot structure of beginning, middle, and end. The beginning we will now call Act One. What do you need to include in your description of this act to start fleshing out your story?

The first thing to do to help answer this question is go back to our logline and premise both of which start with a description of the main character. In Act One, you must define who the story is about—who is the hero or main character or protagonist (whichever wording works best for you) of your script? And you should describe what their flaw is (their inner need). Keep the description very simple, just like in your logline.

As an example, let us look at the logline we wrote for THE WIZARD OF OZ: *A naive Kansas farm girl transported by a terrifying tornado to a magical land must evade the evil witch now hunting her as she embarks on a dangerous journey to find the mysterious wizard who has the power to send her back home.* We could describe Act One like this then: *A naïve Kansas farm girl desperately wants to leave her dreary Depression era life behind for a place "where troubles melt like lemon drops."* That sets up the main character (farm girl Dorothy), and her flaw (she's naïve enough to think that a place like that actually exists), as well as the world she inhabits (Depression era Kansas).

Now we know who we're following, and what her flaw is. We need to transition this set up into action though, to get us into Act Two. Remember our heroine should be proactive. She should have to act to achieve a goal. To push the story into Act Two, we first need to introduce Dorothy's goal. What does she want? And what choice does she have to make to get what she wants? And who or what will try to stop her from getting this? To answer that, let's add some stuff from the logline to the first act: *Her wish is seemingly granted when a terrifying tornado transports Dorothy to the magical land of Oz, but in doing so it drops her and her house on top of the Wicked Witch of the East, killing her.*

Once our farm girl lands in this magical place, she immediately realizes that she has a huge problem. Her wish just led to someone's death, and that someone has a sister, the Wicked Witch of the West, and this witch is pissed. Not only has Dorothy killed her sister, but she's also upset the **status quo** of Oz, becoming a hero to little Munchkins everywhere for disposing of their oppressor. For that, the Wicked Witch wants Dorothy dead. The only way to avoid this terrible fate, she is told, is to follow the Yellow Brick Road to the Emerald City, and when she gets there to ask the Wizard, the ruler of all Oz, to send her home safely to Kansas. Otherwise she's toast. Let's add the following then to finish out Act One: After being hailed a hero and being given the dead witch's ruby red slippers, Dorothy's life is threatened by the Wicked Witch of the West, the vengeful sister of the dead witch. To save herself, Dorothy must head off on a journey to the Emerald City to find the Wizard of Oz and ask him to use his magical powers to send her home safely to Kansas. Our Act One description would finally then read thusly:

A naïve Kansas farm girl desperately wants to leave her dreary Depression era life behind for a place "where troubles melt like lemon drops." Her wish is seemingly granted when a terrifying tornado transports her to the magical land of Oz, but the twister drops her and her house on top of the Wicked Witch of the East, killing her. After being hailed a hero and being given the dead witch's ruby red slippers, Dorothy's life is then threatened by the Wicked Witch of the West, the vengeful sister of the dead witch, and Dorothy is forced to head off on a journey to the Emerald City to find the Wizard of Oz and ask him to use his magical powers to send her home safely to Kansas—if she wants to remain alive.

We could tighten this description up, making it shorter and a little less detailed if we wanted, or we could add some more details to further flesh things out, but for now, it's good enough. We have our character, her problem, and the stakes (life or death).

Time to move on to the second act, wherein our heroine must struggle mightily to achieve her goal, to get what she wants—which is the Wizard to send her home safely. This Act Two struggle should ideally be a confrontation with an antagonistic force, a villain, that builds in intensity, rising in action until it reaches the end of the second act—the climactic battle between heroine and villainess. We know the villain is the Wicked Witch, and we know Dorothy's goal, so this conflict shouldn't be too hard to describe. Looking back at the end of the logline, we could take what we wrote there and develop it into something like this:

Following the advice of Glinda the Good Witch of the North, Dorothy sets off on the Yellow Brick Road in her new red shoes to find the mysterious Wizard of Oz, the only one she's told who has the power to get her safely back home. She must evade the evil witch now hunting her as she embarks on this dangerous journey, and to help her cause she picks up several allies on the way who share her fear of the Witch. She makes it to the Emerald City, barely, but when she arrives the Wizard tells her he will only help her if she brings him the broom of the nasty old witch. Desperate to get home, she and her allies attempt to fulfill the Wizard's high price, but the Wicked Witch outwits Dorothy and captures her, locking her up in a dungeon, where everything now appears totally hopeless for our heroine.

Again, we could add more detail to this, or trim it down, but we really don't need to at this point. For the purposes of going from 1 logline to 3 Acts, we have done enough. We have reached the last turning point, the final confrontation between Dorothy and the Wicked Witch. All that's left is the climax and resolution.

Act Three is usually the easiest act to write. Easiest if you have done all the work leading up to it. In our case, we've done a decent job, so let's finish this story. Trapped in the Witch's lair, Dorothy must resolve her inner need or she will fail to achieve her goal. She must realize that happiness cannot be found by wishing your troubles away, that she must confront trouble, in the form of the evil Wicked Witch, head on, or lose all her new friends, not to mention her life. So, she does just this, and in one desperate final act in which she heroically tries to save one of her allies, our transformed Kansas farm girl douses the villainous Witch in water and lo and behold watches her triumphantly melt away. That is the climax of our narrative, the summit of our pyramid, the climactic moment of the rising action which we built up to through the ever escalating confrontation between our protagonist and antagonist.

We're almost done, now. All we must do is get Dorothy back home again, which was her goal all along. To do that, let's add the following: With the Witch dead, Dorothy takes the broom back to the Wizard, and promptly finds out he's a sham. If she wants to go home, she'll have to do it herself, by clicking her two red slippers together, and wishing as hard to go home as she did to leave way back in Act One. After some tearful goodbyes, and after having finally learned that if you want to find the merry old land of Oz you should look within yourself, she clicks her heels and is whisked magically back home, where she hugs her Aunt and tells everyone within earshot, "There's no place like home." Happy ending achieved, resolution to story arrived at, we can now put it all together in one brief three act summation of our story:

Act One: *A naïve Kansas farm girl desperately wants to leave her dreary Depression era life behind for a place "where troubles melt like lemon drops." Her wish is seemingly granted when a terrifying tornado transports her to the magical land of Oz, but the twister drops her and her house on top of the Wicked Witch of the East, killing her. After being hailed a hero and being given the dead witch's ruby red slippers, Dorothy's life is then threatened by the Wicked Witch of the West, the vengeful sister of the dead witch, and Dorothy is forced to head off on a journey to the Emerald City to find the Wizard of Oz and ask him to use his magical powers to send her home safely to Kansas—if she wants to remain alive.*

Act Two: *Following the advice of Glinda the Good Witch of the North, Dorothy sets off on the yellow brick road in her new red shoes to find the mysterious Wizard of Oz who she is told may have the power to get her safely back home. She must evade the evil witch now hunting her as she embarks on this dangerous journey, and to help her cause she picks up several allies on the way who share her fear of the Witch. She makes it to the Emerald City, barely, but when she arrives the Wizard tells her he will only help her if she brings him the broom of the nasty old witch. Desperate to get home, she and her allies attempt to fulfill the Wizard's high price, but the Wicked Witch outwits Dorothy and captures her, locking her up in a dungeon where everything now appears totally hopeless for our heroine.*

__Act Three:__ Trapped in the Witch's lair, Dorothy finally realizes that happiness cannot be found by wishing your troubles away. She must confront trouble, in the form of the evil Wicked Witch, head on, or lose all her new friends, not to mention her life. So she does just this, and in one desperate final act in which she heroically tries to save one of her allies, our transformed Kansas farm girl douses the villainous Witch in water and lo and behold watches her triumphantly melt away. With the Witch dead, Dorothy takes the broom back to the Wizard, and promptly finds out he's a sham. If she wants to get home, he tells her, she'll have to do it by herself, by clicking her two ruby red slippers together and wishing as hard to go home as she did to leave Kansas at the outset. So, she clicks her heels and wishes withal her might, and she's whisked magically back home, where she hugs her Aunt and tells everyone she loves, "There's no place like home."

STRUCTURE AS ARGUMENT

There is another way to look at three act structure, one that is equally valid and effective in the writing process, and that is to see it as a kind of argument. This is what philosophers call a dialectical model or argument. **Dialectics** was invented by the Ancient Greeks (who I already told you invented everything important) and, surprise surprise, was highly espoused by none other than Aristotle, our man about town for all things structural. A dialectical argument is structured around a confrontation of two opposites called a **thesis** and an **antithesis**. The result of these two ideas butting heads is called a **synthesis**.

In philosophy, this is known as the **dialectical method**, and it can be understood easiest as a debate between two people holding different points of view on a subject but who wish to establish the truth through a reasoned argument. This type of argument has three basic stages of development: first is the thesis, which gives rise to a reaction; then an antithesis, which contradicts or negates the thesis; and finally the confrontation, where the argument is resolved by means of a synthesis, a blending or combing of the two opposites. If you're paying attention, you'll notice how this sounds a little familiar, right? It's not unlike the dramatic narrative structure described by Field and Freytag. David Mamet defined this kind of three act model of story structure as: ORDER—CHAOS—RE-ORDER.

The thesis represents Act One, which in this case is the status quo. The status quo is who the main character is and where we find them, both physically and emotionally, at the beginning of the story. This is **thesis world** of your screenplay structured as argument (*order* in Mamet's terms). The story turns in a new direction at the end of Act One as we've said, and the hero heads into the unknown, a fish out of water, to do battle with the antagonist, as he or she strives to achieve their goal. Think about how often in a movie you see a hero step into a new world, often tentatively at first, after having been knocked off their status quo balance somewhere in the first act. Luke must leave Tatooine in STAR WARS and head off into the big scary galaxy to help Obi Wan Kenobi and Princess Leia defeat Darth Vader and the Evil Empire. Elle must leave the soft, comfortable confines of her LA college sorority life and head to Harvard Law School (talk about a fish out of water!) to find happiness and true love.

The Galactic Empire and Harvard Law School couldn't be more different than the backwater planet Luke grew up on or the wildly pink and prim Los Angeles of Elle's world in Act One. And that's exactly the point. These are what we can call the **antithesis world** with respect of our heroes and heroines, the total opposite of the thesis world they inhabited in the first act (*chaos* in Mamet's terms). These places are polar (dialectical) opposites of the main characters' first act comfort zones. And it's in this conflict of worlds, this polarized difference, this opposition that our characters will have to struggle the most to achieve their goal. That's where, as writers, you want to send your protagonists. Dorothy must go to Oz, dialectically speaking, if we want this story to work. It's within this opposition, in the conflict between thesis and antithesis worlds, that she must resolve her inner need, deal with her character flaw, learn the lesson she needs to learn, so that she can finally confront the antagonist, the Wicked Witch, head on, if she ever hopes to defeat her and get what she wants—in the third act.

THESIS WORLD + ANTITHESIS WORLD = SYNTHESIS WORLD

The third act of many a story is often some kind of blending of the two worlds, a synthesis of Act One and Act Two, that shows us how the conflict was resolved by our hero (*re-order* per Mamet). This dialectic approach starts with who the protagonist is in the thesis world and tests him or her in the antithesis world so that they can become who they need to be to survive and succeed in Act Three, the **synthesis world**.

Many times in movies, this results in the hero returning to where they started, and showing us how they have changed, as in THE WIZARD OF OZ. The young naïve farm girl of Act One who thinks she can solve all life's problems by running away from home, realizes, only by having to journey through a place completely unlike home, that what she thought was wrong. Happiness isn't found somewhere over the rainbow; happiness is where the heart is—inside her all along. Dorothy returns from the technicolor land of Oz to the black and white world of Kansas, but she's changed. She's a different girl now, a better version of her initial self because she's dealt with her flaw, resolved her inner need, and come out of it a new, synthesized Dorothy—a person with courage and full of love for her family and her home. And home no longer looks or feels the same to her. It's somehow different. Better too.

Sometimes the hero ends up in a place that is the blending of the two worlds (Act One and Act Two). In LEGALLY BLONDE, Elle never returns to Los Angeles. Instead we see her win in the court room and then two years later, graduate first in her class. We see in Act Three how she's changed emotionally by telling her former boyfriend she no longer needs him in her life at all. She's perfectly okay without him.

Following is a logline and three act description for THE SILENCE OF THE LAMBS:

Logline: A young, naive FBI cadet must confide in an incarcerated and fiendishly manipulative serial killer in order to get his help catching another serial killer who skins his victims before this killer strikes again.

Act One: A young, naïve FBI cadet, Clarice Starling, is asked to help on a serial murder case. She reluctantly agrees to interview the brilliant, manipulative serial killer Hannibal Lector about the case in order to uncover who the new killer is and how to find him.

Act Two: Hannibal forces Clarice to confide in him if she wants to gain his help, and as she does he gives her important clues to finding the killer. This ultimately leads to Clarice having to confront a terrible trauma from her own childhood, before she finally can uncover the identity of the killer who skins his victims.

Act Three: Clarice confronts the killer and saves his latest intended victim.

As you move forward in the process, and further develop your script from 3 Acts to sequences and scenes, remember to construct a second act world which will test your main character to the limits of their abilities to change, adapt, and grow. It will help you construct the vessel into which your character arc can develop and flow naturally. And this will help you turn what was just an idea for a movie into a good, maybe even great, screenplay.

When you have finished creating the basic structure of your story, going from logline to three act description, using whichever of these two methods you chose, you should have a story that is approximately a half page to one page long. Remember to keep it as short and succinct as possible. Doing so will force you to keep your story simple. As you move forward, you may come back to this three act description and modify it, just as you might modify your single sentence logline, depending on what issues come up as you move forward in the process. Writing a screenplay isn't always a straight-line journey. You can and often will take two steps forward and one step back. Don't get discouraged. Trust the process, and master it. It will pay great dividends in the long run.

One last thing about three act structure. You'll find people out there who argue that this structure isn't cinematic, that it's too constraining, that it doesn't always, every single time, describe the basic plot of a movie. You'll hear arguments for more acts or fewer, as the best way to structure a screenplay. Feel free to listen to them, if you like, but know this. If you want to learn how to write a screenplay, if you want to understand screenwriting, you better learn three act structure. For every movie someone can name that supposedly doesn't follow this basic structure, I can name a hundred that do. The evidence is overwhelming in this argument.

Once you understand this structure, and once you've written half-a-dozen screenplays using it, then you can start to think about other ways to structure a film. Until then, do yourself a huge favor and learn three act structure inside and out. It may look simple, but like the logline it's not as easy to do right off the bat as you might think. Like writing a great logline, constructing a good three act structure takes practice, thought, patience, and hard work.

EXERCISES

Exercise 1: Take your favorite loglines for three of the movie ideas you developed in the Chapter Three exercises and expand each of them into a three act story. Make sure you have a clear beginning, middle, and end. Be as brief as possible with your act descriptions.

FURTHER READINGS

Poetics by Aristotle
Screenplay by Syd Field

Expanding
3 Acts into
8 Sequences

The next step in the process is to turn our 3 Acts into 8 Sequences. But before we do that we need to digress a moment and ask a simple question: **Why are most movies around two hours long?** According to Hitchcock, the answer is simple: "The length of a film," he said in his uniquely droll manner, "should be directly related to the endurance of the human bladder." To answer the question a different way, feature length movies are between 80 and 120 minutes long because that's how long people like them to be.

This "standard" movie length developed rather quickly in the history of film, and by the 1920s, with the advent of sound, which introduced dialogue into movie scripts, it became pretty much set in stone. When sound entered the picture in 1927 with THE JAZZ SINGER, Hollywood producers turned to the one source for dialogue writers that they knew well—playwrights. These writers brought many theatrical conventions to screenwriting, and act breaks were one of them. As Hollywood became more industrialized in its production of films, the length of a movie script and the formatting became fairly standardized.

Written in standard screenplay format (which we will discuss in Part Two), one page of script equals about one minute of a movie, so a 90-minute movie will be based on a 90-page script, give or take a page or two. The vast majority of feature films fall into the 80- to 120-minute time length. There's always exception of course, like the movie ALL IS LOST with Robert Redford which only has one line of dialogue in 106 minutes of film and is roughly 40 pages in length because of that. Aaron Sorkin's MOLLY'S GAME has a script that's 182 pages long for a movie that runs 134 minutes. These are outliers however.

Teleplays (scripts written for television shows) differ in length from feature film scripts as most TV shows run 30 or 60 minutes long, give or take commercial interruptions, so their structure will necessarily be a little different. This doesn't mean they don't have acts and sequences, just that the sequences are fewer. For our purposes, we're focusing here on **feature film** screenplays. The standard script length is 80–120 minutes long (again based on the one page of script to one minute of film ratio) and this length dictates in some important ways the way a script must be structured, as that structure must work for that time/page length.

One important factor in the development of feature film story structure began in the early days of cinema, and lasted right up until the start of the 21st century: movies were projected on film. Up until just recently, an entire feature length film was delivered to theaters in the form of **reels**.

In the early days of cinema, theaters employed only one projector, and so the projectionist would have to continually switch reels until all eight (for a feature length film) were shown, and the movie was finished. This switching was occasionally clunky, and producers knew this could be a problem for audiences, so they along with the early screenplay writers built fade outs and fade ins to the end of the reels to hide the changeover.

Like the drawing of the curtain to symbolically show the audience the act of a play was over, the momentary darkness brought about by the changing of the reels became a kind of natural structural break in films. Each reel of a film was about 10–15 minutes in length, so if you do the math you can see that it takes eight reels to make an 80- to 120-minute long film. Eventually technological improvements to film projection alleviated this clunky changeover problem, but by then eight reels had become standard, along with the eight sequences of a movie script. Sequences, then, seem to have emerged rather organically over time as cinema developed from shorts to single reel movies to feature length films.

This story of reels-to-sequences I heard told by one **Frank Daniel** in his now legendary script analysis class at USC film school. Daniel used it to explain to his writing students the reason why "sequences" in a film came to be understood as each being about 10–15 pages long. Daniel served as dean of both USC and AFI film schools, and he is also in many ways the godfather of the sequence approach to screenwriting. He taught it to me and to a cadre of other film students who then went out and preached the gospel of screen story structure according to Frank. Daniel taught screenwriting at some of the world's most prestigious film schools, including USC and AFI, along with Columbia, the Sundance Screenwriters Lab and FAMU, and the Prague Academy of Performing Arts. If all those accomplishments weren't enough, he was also the first non-Russian to study at Moscow's famed Gerasimov Institute (the oldest film school in the world). If you know your film history, this is where Kuleshov, Eisenstein and Pudovkin all cut their teeth as film-makers and theoreticians. Daniel's screenwriting acumen is unquestionably great.

Parts of the story Daniel told of this development may be somewhat apocryphal, but the sequence method has proven to hold up quite well over time. Daniel showed over and over again, to students and filmmakers, by analyzing dozens and hundreds of feature length films of all **genres**, that sequences were a very good way for screenwriters to break down the monumental task of creating a feature length screen story by dividing the task into eight distinct parts. To top it all off, Daniel showed that these eight sequences correspond very nicely to basic three-act structure. The First Act has two sequences, the Second Act has four sequences, and the Third Act has two. Simple enough, right? So let's look more closely at this sequence paradigm, as it is sometimes called, to better understand how the sequences work.

THE 8 SEQUENCES DEFINED

The 8 Sequences that make up the next level of structure in film writing, with great deference to Mr. Daniel, are the following:

1. Setup & Catalyst
2. Debate & Decision
3. First Steps into the New World
4. Clarifying the Problem & the Midpoint
5. The Push Back
6. All Appears Lost
7. Applying the Lesson Learned & the Climax
8. Achieving the Goal

To detail this further, let's define these eight sequences and show how they fit into a three-act structure.

Act One

1. *Setup*. In this sequence, you introduce the main character and their status quo, or thesis world. Who is our hero and what is their flaw? This sequence ends with a *catalyst*, an inciting incident (also called a point of attack), which introduces the problem (the goal) to the hero.
2. *Debate & Decision*. Once the problem shows up, the hero, now knocked off balance, struggles to deal with the change in his or her status quo. Often

because of their flaw, they struggle to come up with reasons why they don't/ can't/shouldn't/won't take on the problem. This narrative tension coalesces until he or she is forced, reluctantly, to confront the problem head on, that is to seek to achieve the goal. This is a major turning point in the story, and it's certainly the most easily recognized one by audiences.

Act Two

3. *First Steps into the New World.* Once the hero decides to go after the goal, the story has taken a significant turn. Audiences feel this turn, because they now have something (and someone) to root for. Our hero has chosen, albeit after getting a hard shove, to leave the safety and comfort of their status quo/thesis world to undertake the effort to get what they want, to achieve their goal, in a brand-new world that they are unfamiliar with. The dramatic question the audience is presented with is, will he or she succeed or fail? The protagonist then gets to work, often recruiting allies. But the hero, being human, looks for the easy road at this point, choosing the logical, obvious method to get what they want. Hoping for a quick resolution, their first rather lame effort instead fails completely.

4. *Clarifying the Problem.* Shocked by their failure to easily solve the problem or achieve the goal, to get what they want the hero moves toward a more direct confrontation with the antagonist, which ends in the hero's failure again, at the hands of the villain, at the story's *midpoint.*

    This confrontation often occurs in what Joseph Campbell, author of the seminal book on the structure of myths, *The Hero with a Thousand Faces,* calls the **darkest cave.** "The cave you fear to enter holds the treasure you seek," is a quote often attributed to Campbell but which has its roots in Carl Jung's works on psychology. Jung and Campbell were huge proponents of the power of myths. They believed myths were the stories that we humans tell ourselves over and over that bind societies and cultures together.

    As a screenwriter, this sequence is where you bring the protagonist to his or her darkest cave, to confront the thing they fear most. This isn't literally a cave, usually, but you'd be surprised how often it looks or feels like one in the movies. In THE EMPIRE STRIKES BACK, Luke Skywalker literally enters a cave, this one under a mystical tree at his mentor Yoda's urging. The darkest cave is metaphorically speaking a place where our hero is at their most frightened or vulnerable, but also a place which holds the key in some way to achieving their goal. This confrontation doesn't usually end well, but it is a critical moment for the hero in that they learn something valuable, or gain something useful that will help them succeed, even though they often do not recognize that valuable thing right away. The key thing for Luke in his journey to become a Jedi in THE EMPIRE STRIKES BACK is to understand that he and the evil Darth Vader are connected, that they are somehow one in the same. Of course, we all know how that turns out later on.

This encounter in the darkest cave marks the **midpoint** of the story. The hero, shaken by the encounter, licks his or her wounds, but has learned something of value in the confrontation with the antagonist, something that often *clarifies* how they will eventually have to solve *the problem*, achieve the goal, get what they want. This midpoint often mirrors the climax, in that what will eventually occur in the climax is the opposite of what has just occurred at the midpoint. But because the hero hasn't resolved their inner need yet, they are not yet ready to implement this knowledge to positive effect. They aren't ready to really change. They have not learned the lesson yet.

5. *The Push Back.* Unfortunately for our hero, their first direct confrontation with the villain has now aroused the forces of antagonism, and focused them on our hero. The villain may send henchmen, or take other nefarious steps to push back against the hero's actions. This conflict leads to a further rising of tension. Sometimes, a major **twist**, a **reversal** or betrayal, occurs here, calling into question everything the hero thought they knew before it.

6. *All Appears Lost.* This latest reversal of fortunes causes the hero to sink to an emotional low point, frustrated at his failures, feeling utterly defeated. The villain is winning and our hero wants to throw in the towel and give up. This sequence often ends with some kind of metaphorical or visually symbolic death. It is also the point of maximum tension, because the audience fears that the hero they have become attached to and followed through three-fourth of the story, is about to fail. It looks like they aren't going to get what the audience wants them to get.

Act Three

7. *Applying the Lesson.* Heroes wouldn't be heroes if they just gave up though. Instead, the protagonist musters up the courage and energy to make one more attempt to achieve their goal. And importantly, they finally integrate

the lesson that the antithesis world of the second act has been trying to teach them, often through the knowledge they gained at the midpoint, to resolve their inner need. Lesson learned, the hero girds himself for a final battle with the villain resulting in the climax, the direct confrontation between the protagonist and the antagonist. One of them wins, the other loses.

8. *Achieving the Goal.* If this story has a happy ending, and most Hollywood movies do, the hero has now achieved their goal, got what they wanted. (If he or she didn't learn their lesson, or learned it too late, and were defeated by the antagonist in the climax, we'd have a classical tragedy like *Hamlet* on our hands). In the aftermath of their victory, the hero then gets the spoils of their hard-earned achievement, and balance is restored in the world, albeit a new balance, a synthesis of thesis and antithesis. We often see this new balance, the new status quo for our changed forever hero, in the *denouement* which brings the story to a close.

Example: *The Secret Life of Walter Mitty*

One of my favorite movies, and favorite scripts, of the last few years is *The Secret Life of Walter Mitty* written by Steven Conrad and directed by Ben Stiller. I'm a sucker for movies like this, probably because I identify strongly with the hero, but also because the movie is so beautifully structured. Let's examine how this film might look broken down into eight sequences:

Act One

1. *Setup.* In this sequence, we are introduced to Walter Mitty, a negative assets manager at Life magazine who daydreams of adventures and has a crush on a co-worker named Cheryl. Mitty works with a famous photojournalist, Sean O'Connell, who sends Mitty his latest set of negatives and a wallet as a gift in appreciation of Mitty's work. O'Connell believes negative #25 captures the "quintessence" of Life, and that it should be used for the cover of the magazine's final print issue as it converts to online status. The negative however is missing from the set, sending Walter into a panic (catalyst, inciting incident).

2. *Debate & Decision.* Walter is forced to stall for time with corporate transition manager Ted Hendricks (the antagonist of this story), who is handling the downsizing. While sitting outside Life's office viewing the other negatives Sean sent, Cheryl approaches Mitty and suggests that he think of the negatives as clues to Sean's location. They look at three of them, including one of

a person's thumb with a unique ring on it, and another of a curved piece of wood. A third picture of a boat leads Mitty to determine that O'Connell is in Greenland. At first, he's unsure what to do, but desperate to find the negative, he reluctantly hops on a plane and flies there to look for Sean.

Act Two

3. *First Steps into the New World.* Now in Greenland (the complete antithesis of New York), Walter makes his first attempt to solve the problem of the missing negative. Here he meets a bartender at the airport who tells him that O'Connell left a day before on a ship. To find him, Mitty will need to go on the postal helicopter, and the pilot is drunk. Walter tries to convince the helicopter pilot to help him, but the drunken man only wants to drown his romantic sorrows in beer. The two men end up in a brawl, and just before he is pummeled to death, Mitty recognizes the pilot's thumb is adorned with the unique ring he saw in one of Sean's negatives. He now realizes he is on the right track.

4. *Clarifying the Problem.* But the pilot is very drunk, and Walter is afraid to get in the helicopter with him. Then he imagines Cheryl singing David Bowie's "Space Oddity", and this gives him courage. He makes a last-minute dash and boards the helicopter. As they near the ship, Mitty learns the helicopter cannot land upon it. Misunderstanding the pilot, instead of jumping into a dinghy boat that's there to catch him, Mitty takes a crazy leap of faith and jumps for the main vessel. But he misses it and falls in the ocean. He splashes down into ice-cold, shark-infested waters, losing a box of ship-to-shore radio components before finally being brought aboard.

5. *The Push Back.* On the ship, Mitty learns that O'Connell left the ship a day earlier. The crew offers him some clementine cake O'Connell left behind; Mitty discovers O'Connell's destinations in the cake's wrapping paper. The itinerary directs Mitty to Iceland, where O'Connell is photographing the volcano Eyjafjallajökull. He arrives at the local village of Skógar near the volcano using a skateboard, and notices O'Connell on the plane flying near the volcano. An eruption forces Mitty to flee, and as there is nothing else he can do, he obeys a text message from Ted recalling him to New York.

6. *All Appears Lost.* For failing to recover the negative, his first failure in a long career with the magazine, Mitty is fired by Hendricks. He also learns that

Cheryl, who was let go earlier, seems to have reconciled with her estranged husband. Mitty returns home discouraged and visits his mother, throwing away the wallet he received from O'Connell. This latest reversal of fortunes causes the hero to sink to an emotional low point, feeling utterly defeated.

Act Three

7. *Applying the Lesson.* As he wallows in despair, Mitty recognizes the curve of the piano in his mother's house is one of the images in Sean's last negatives. When asked, Mitty's mom mentions that she met O'Connell. She had told Mitty before but he was daydreaming and failed to hear her. This information leads Mitty to discover that O'Connell is in the Himalayas.

   There he finds Sean photographing a rare snow leopard. When asked about the negative, O'Connell explains that the message he left Walter on the gift wrapping to "look inside" was literal; the negative was in the wallet. Unfortunately, Mitty had misinterpreted this message. When pressed to reveal what the image on the negative was, O'Connell dismisses the question and joins in a high-altitude football game with some locals. Mitty flies to Los Angeles thinking he has failed in his quest, but somehow realizing he has found something else, the courage to act on his dreams, in the journey.

8. *Achieving the Goal.* While helping his mother sell her piano, Mitty recounts his story with Sean and the negative to his mom, but mentions he does not have the wallet anymore. His mother says she always keeps his knickknacks and gives him the wallet that she retrieved from the trash. Inside the wallet Walter finds a small manila envelope the size of a single-frame 35mm negative. An emboldened Mitty delivers the missing negative to Life magazine, tells management that it was the photograph O'Connell wanted for the final issue, and berates Hendricks for disrespecting the staff that made the magazine so honored before walking away from the office for the last time.

   Mitty reunites with Cheryl, and with his newfound confidence and courage tells her that he has been inspired by her, and then learns that Cheryl's ex-husband was only at her house to repair the refrigerator. Mitty tells Cheryl of his adventures and admits that he still does not know what negative #25 shows. Mitty and Cheryl see the final issue of Life at a newsstand, with its cover dedicated to the staff. It is accompanied by the photograph from negative #25, showing Mitty sitting outside of the Life building, examining a contact sheet. Mitty and Cheryl then walk down the street holding hands clearly ready to embark on a new adventure, together.

THE FAIRYTALE METHOD

There's another way to break a script into 8 sequences using the structure of fairytales. Brian McDonald, in his book *Invisible Ink*, claims that all effective stories are structured, like fairy tales, in this way:

Once upon a time...
And every day...
Until one day...
And because of this...
And because of this...
And because of this...
Until finally...
And ever since that day...

Using THE WIZARD OF OZ as an example, this fairytale approach would yield the following structure:

Once upon a time there lived a Kansas farm girl named Dorothy.

And every day Dorothy dreamed of leaving the farm for a happier, trouble-free place, somewhere over the rainbow.

Until one day, her farm house was caught up in a tornado that blew Dorothy and her little dog Toto all the way to the magical land of Oz where it landed on a witch, killing her.

And because of this, Dorothy became a hero to the munchkins who hated the witch and was given the witch's ruby red slippers, but she also became a mortal enemy of the dead witch's evil sister.

And because of this she was desperate to return home, so she followed the yellow brick road to the Emerald City, as she was instructed, all the while dodging the wicked witch, and found the Wizard of Oz, who told Dorothy he would send her back home if she brought back to him the wicked witch's broom.

And because of this Dorothy went to the witch's lair, but instead of getting the broom she was captured by the witch who locked Dorothy up in a tower. And there she tearfully realized she might never see her Kansas home and her beloved Aunt Em ever again.

Until finally, Dorothy confronted the witch directly when she threatened to burn her friend the Scarecrow, dousing the nasty witch in water and causing her to melt into a puddle of nothing. She then took the witch's broom to the Wizard, who told her he really couldn't help her, and that she alone had the power to return home, if only she wished for it strongly enough. So, Dorothy wished with all her heart and was transported home...

And ever since that day she has lived happily on the farm back in Kansas, knowing in her heart that there's no place like home.

Many movies can be laid out in this way, but the correspondence isn't always exactly one to one with the sequence approach. It is close enough though, so that if you do choose to use the fairytale method you can easily convert it into the eight sequences needed in our process.

There are a couple things to note, however. First, the debate isn't always clear in the fairytale method, and not just in this example. If you know your OZ, you clearly remember that when Dorothy first decides to run away from home she meets Prof. Marvel, and ends up turning back (after retrieving Toto from the nasty Ms. Gulch). She has real doubts about heeding her call to adventure, but fate has other things in store for our heroine. Dorothy must literally be blown off her status quo, that of the naïve young farm girl, by a tornado before she can take the first step of her journey to wisdom following the Yellow Brick Road.

Note also, that the first two parts of the fairytale method are both setup, so you must be careful not to turn them into two separate sequences—they both occur in the first sequence, *before* the catalyst (*Until one day...*) or inciting incident. In THE WIZARD OF OZ, this catalyst or point of attack is Miss Gulch's seizing of Dorothy's dog Toto. That incident disrupts Dorothy's status quo, and eventually forces her into the antithesis world of Oz (in all its Technicolor glory) and into action to achieve a goal (to get back home, with or without the Wizard's help).

One strength of this fairytale method is that most of us are familiar with fairy-tales, and we understand, consciously or subconsciously, how they work as stories. We get the structure of them, we feel the rhythm of the tale. Another, less obvious, strength of this approach is that it clearly shows the way the parts of the story *connect. Until one day... And because of this... Until finally... And ever since...*

These phrases act as linkages that connect what happens first to what happens next. They help give your story a logical flow, and that is a very important thing. The sequence paradigm also reinforces the linkage between events. It creates a logical flow to the story that needs to be there for the audience to maintain interest in the outcome. If you want the audience to care what happens to your hero, they must believe that what is happening is real, even though it was all made up in your head. Creating a story with a logical flow, which sequencing can help you do, will keep the audience focused on the dramatic question every movie proposes: will our hero(ine) succeed or not?

This necessity for the sequences to feel linked brings up one of the potential pitfalls of using any kind of formula or process in art. The danger is that when you do things in pieces, those pieces don't always add up to a whole, or ideally to more than the sum of the individual parts. A movie like SCOTT PILGRIM VS THE WORLD to my mind illustrates this problem. Despite receiving some decent reviews from critics for its visual style and sense of humor, the film tanked at the box office, where it grossed only $47.7 million against a production budget of reportedly $85–90 million. $47 million might sound great to you or me, but studios and production companies are rarely happy with this type of poor return on their investment.

In this case, it seems that audiences didn't respond to the film well enough to make it a hit, and this was likely the result of a weak narrative structure. The sequences didn't tie together well enough to keep the audience engaged in Scott's story. We stopped caring what happens to Scott because the threads didn't connect. He battles one of his ex-girlfriend's ex-boyfriends, then another, then another. There is no real build, no emotional growth from one confrontation to the next, so the film ends up with a very episodic structure: first this happens, then this, then that. No flow to the story, just a series of starts and stops. Audiences tend to lose the emotional thread of a story in cases like this, and thus lose interest in what happens to the hero. The sequence paradigm and the fairytale structure method of developing those sequences help you avoid this problem by forcing you to think about how the various parts are linked together. This happens *because* that happened, which results in this happening. The key to using the fairytale method, if you choose to use it, is to make sure you eventually turn your fairytale structure into an eight-sequence description. You'll need to do that to move on to the next step in the process.

EXERCISES

Exercise 1: Break down one (and preferably all) of the following movies into 8 sequences:

> *Casablanca*
> *Ordinary People*
> *Aliens*
> *Toy Story*
> *Get Out*

Exercise 2: Now break them down again, using the fairytale method. Note where you see differences in the two methods, and think about why those differences are there, and how you might resolve them.

Exercise 3: Using one of the loglines that you have developed into 3 Acts, answer the following questions:

a. *Who is the hero whose actions and choices are going to drive the story forward?*

b. *What does this protagonist want? What primary desire is forcing them to take action?*

c. *Why does he or she want it so much? What's going to happen if he or she DOESN'T get it? Define the STAKES of your story.*

d. *What are the obstacles? Who is the antagonist, or what is the antagonistic force that is keeping the protagonist from getting what they want?*

Exercise 4: Using the fairytale structure method, break this three act story of yours into 8 sequences.

1. Once upon a time...
2. And every day...
3. Until one day...
4. And because of this...
5. And because of this...
6. And because of this...
7. Until finally...
8. And ever since that day...

FURTHER READINGS:

Screenwriting: The Sequence Approach by Paul Gulino

Invisible Ink by Brian McDonald.

From 8 Sequences to 16 Major Story Beats

Movies are like music—they gotta have rhythm. And the king of understanding rhythm in the world of screenwriting is **Blake Snyder**. Snyder was a Hollywood screenwriter, script consultant, author, and teacher. His *Save The Cat!* book on screenwriting and story structure is one of the most popular books on screenwriting ever written. In the film industry today, it's almost a bible, and one of the few books on screenwriting, or any subject, that nearly all Hollywood producers, agents, and studio executives have read.

Snyder loved Hollywood movies. The word "commercial" was not an epithet to him, but the sign that a movie could connect with an audience. For Snyder, all Hollywood movies were genre films, so all films could be characterized as being of one type or another (and for him there were 10 genres, and only 10). He isn't the only writing guru to believe there are only a set number of story types or plots (some say there are 7, some 20). What really set Snyder's approach apart from all the others, from Aristotle to Syd Field to Frank Daniel, was what has become known as the **Blake Snyder Beat Sheet**.

For Snyder, this beat sheet is the key step in going from a three act story to a complete feature screenplay. He proposed that there are fifteen beats in every screen story, and he even listed the page or pages of the script where they belonged. They are the following:

1. Opening Image (page 1)
2. Theme Stated (page 2)
3. Set-up (page 1–10)
4. Catalyst (12)
5. Debate (12–25)
6. Break into Act Two (25)

7. B Story (30)
8. Fun and Games (30–55)
9. Midpoint (55)
10. Bad Guys Close In (55–75)
11. All Is Lost (75)
12. Dark Night of the Soul (75–85)
13. Break into Act Three (85)
14. Finale (85–110)
15. Final Image (110)

Snyder's beat sheet is the work of a genius of story structure, and so it only makes sense to include beats, though with some slight modifications and one addition, in our 1-3-8-16-40 screenwriting process.

THE 16 STORY BEATS OF A SCREENPLAY DEFINED

With a deep bow of deference to the late, great, and highly influential Mr. Snyder, I propose that there are 16 major beats to a screenplay, not 15, and that they are these:

1. The Opening (page 1)
2. The Status Quo (beginning about page 2 or 3)

3. The Catalyst (somewhere between page 12 and 15)
4. Doubt, debate, decision. (beginning around page 13–16)

5. Entering the New World (beginning around page 25–30)
6. Find Some Allies and... (between page 25 and 35)

7. Try Again, But Harder This Time (between page 35/45 and 50/55)
8. Clarify the Problem (somewhere between page 50 and 60)

9. The Forces of Antagonism Respond (beginning around page 55–60)
10. The Hero Retreats (around page 60–65)

11. Things Look So Bleak (between pages 70 and 90)
12. Metaphorically Dead (occurs somewhere around page 75–90)

13. Having Learned the Lesson (beginning around page 75–90)
14. Once More into the Breach (between page 80 and 100)

15. The Final Confrontation (somewhere in pages 85–110)

16. The Takeaway (the final page or two of the script)

The first four beats constitute Act One (pages 1 to 25/30). The next 8 beats make up Act Two (pages 25/30 to pages 75/90). And the last 4 make up Act Three (pages 75/90 to pages 80/120). Each of these beats has a specific function, just like the 8 sequences you created. You'll notice that where these beats come (what page number) can vary slightly, because the length of a movie isn't exact, but as we said varies from 80 to 120 minutes or so. The beats can also be divided up into sequences and described in a bit more detail, so that the overall the structure of a script outlined as sixteen beats would look like this:

Act One
Sequence 1

1. *The Opening* (pg. 1). Whereas Snyder proposes an opening image, scripts are constructed of scenes, and a single image rarely conveys much meaning out of context whether in the script or the finished film. So instead of an opening image, we need an opening beat, one or two scenes, to get the story going. This first story beat of a film is crucial to setting the **tone** of the movie. Is it going to be funny, scary, a tear-jerker? What kind of scary or funny? Audiences want to know what to expect over the next two hours, and this scene tells them. The opening scene in many ways sets the rules for the audience. It should also ideally hook the audience, and begin drawing them into the story. This first beat sometimes also highlights the hero's inner need or flaw in some way, though that more often happens in the next beat. This opening usually has little if anything to do with the overall plot (the goal, what the character wants to achieve).

Think of the classic opening scene of RAIDERS OF THE LOST ARK, screenplay by the very talented Lawrence Kasdan. It's the perfect example of the power and utility of an opening scene. It tells the audience hang on to your seats, you're in for a roller-coaster ride in an action adventure period piece, and it's going to be a whole lot of fun. It doesn't introduce us to the main plot, the search for the Ark, but it does tell the audience a lot about what kind of movie they are about to see. The opening also should give the audience a hint, more than a hint ideally, of who the protagonist is. In RAIDERS, we learn a lot about Indy in the opening, including what his biggest fear is (snakes), and who his nemesis might be (Belloq). The opening also lets the audience know that Jones is obsessed with uncovering ancient artifacts at almost any cost, and is willing to risk life and limb, his and others, to get these treasures. This opening hooks the audience from the get go, and its success led to RAIDERS becoming one of the all-time biggest box office hits in film history.

2. *The Status Quo World* (page 2 to page 12–15). Once you've clued the audience in to what type of movie this is you are writing, you need to establish the status quo world of the main character. Where is your hero in the world, not just physically but just as importantly emotionally and psychologically, at the outset? You set up this status quo so the audience can get familiar with the surroundings in the story, and to better know who they will be rooting for in the context of those surroundings. Done right, this second beat begins to emotionally connect the audience to the protagonist. Remember that you are setting up the status quo of the hero in the first sequence, showing the place where they have grown comfortable, so that in a moment, you can knock them off balance, disrupt their status quo, with the incident that incites the overall plot—the **catalyst**.

This second beat is where we also often reveal to the audience what the main character's flaw is, what the inner need is that they must resolve before they will ever succeed. This flaw is what will help create a rounded, believable protagonist.

In RAIDERS, this is the beat that introduces us to the world of Indiana Jones, the nerdy but handsome professor of archeology. We already learned he's a daring adventurer from the opening scene, but we connect with him more deeply, more emotionally when we see how his students crush on him, and how he's befuddled, almost embarrassed by their adoration. In fact, he's downright afraid of that emotional stuff, of genuine human, romantic connection, of love, as we will soon learn. This is Indy's flaw. He knows how to death-defyingly swing from a whip over a bottomless pit, but he has no idea how to deal with a woman on an emotional level, especially a woman he loves.

This second beat is also often, as Snyder and others point out, where the **theme** or **dramatic question** of the story is stated. In movies with long opening scenes, the theme will often appear there to illustrate the main character's flaw, or state the stories dramatic question. In other films, it will appear during the status quo set up. "[S]omeone (usually *not* the main character) will pose a question or make a statement (usually *to* the main character) that is the theme of the movie," Snyder states.

In dialectical terms, (with story as argument) the **dramatic question** (called the **premise**) is stated here, and then, as Snyder explains, "the rest of the screenplay is the argument laid out, either proving or disproving the [premise]." In other words, the thesis world (set up in Act One) argues or conflicts with the antithesis world (Act Two), and the result is a resolution or synthesis of these two points of view that answers the dramatic question, or in other terms, proves or disproves the thematic premise. This may sound very theoretical, but the point is a simple one. *Here in this beat is where you clue the audience in as to what the story is about.* You're telling them why they should care by posing a question to them. It's a subtle but very effective way to keep the audience hooked.

Many genre films don't bother stating the theme directly. In fact, it's more likely the theme will have to be inferred by the audience, often from the dramatic question that is posed. It isn't always obvious to the audience right away, or to the main character, but the theme, stated or inferred, plants the seed in the audience's mind of what a movie is going to be about. Snyder's point is that "a good movie has to be 'about something'", and this beat is where to address that notion.

The theme is not always articulated in this beat though, and it's important to note this, because one of the dangers of adhering too strictly to any formula is that it's easy to point out real-world examples that contradict it. With respect to where the theme or dramatic question is posed, for example, in RAIDERS it doesn't occur until Marcus Brody articulates the basic theme, be careful what you wish for, in the fourth story beat (*Doubt, debate, decision*), when he warns Indy to be careful because going after the Ark will be unlike anything he's ever attempted. In THE WIZARD OF OZ, the theme, the dramatic question, is sung in the *Status Quo* beat by Dorothy when she sings *Somewhere Over the Rainbow*: "*Why oh why can't I [find happiness]?*" In WHEN HARRY MET SALLY, we hear the theme spoken out loud early in the story by Billy Crystal (who *is* the main character, just to show you that you can bend a "rule", without breaking it): "*Men and women cannot be friends because the sex part always gets in the way.*"

It's good to be aware that there is some flexibility to where the theme, or the dramatic question, may be stated, and how. This flexibility opens the door for writers to be more creative and not so formulaic in their writing (we will discuss this point further in Chapter Six and in Part Two). The key thing that must be done in this second story beat is to establish the status quo world of the movie for the audience, letting them know who the story is about (the protagonist) and where that protagonist is emotionally, psychologically, and physically (what is their flaw). You're telling the audience here is the hero in all his flawed reality and here's their comfort zone, and you do this because in the next moment, you are going to flip the hero's apple cart, and upset their status quo forever.

Sequence 2

3. *The Catalyst* (somewhere between page 12 and 15). The catalyst is the moment that begins to turn the story in a new direction, toward the main plot. Ideally, the catalyst comes out of the blue, an unexpected incident that really surprises or shocks the hero, knocking them completely off balance emotionally. In other words, it upsets the status quo world of the protagonist that you set up in the previous two beats. This unexpected event plays into an important element of human nature. Most people don't like to witness, let alone experience undeserved suffering. Nor do they like their comfortable, well-regulated lives, disrupted. But life has a way of bringing change into our otherwise mundane, predictable lives in completely unexpected ways that bring about real suffering. It's how we react to this sudden change in our circumstance, to this suffering, that defines our character. And it's how writers can define their hero's character for the audience.

In RAIDERS, the shock of surprise is delivered to Dr. Jones when the military informs him that the Nazi's are hot on the trail of the mythical, all-powerful Ark of the Covenant. It also sets the stakes, very high again, when Jones states what the others fear—that if the Nazis get the Ark, they will be able to use it as a weapon to take over the world. This moment is Indy's call to adventure. The question now is will Dr. Jones heed that call or not? Will he join the fight against the Nazis or remain comfortably hidden away in his college office?

In the movie DALLAS BUYERS CLUB, the catalyst happens in the scene in which the protagonist, hell-raising heterosexual cowboy Ron Woodruff, is told he has AIDS and will die from it within thirty days. This devastating news knocks the homophobic Ron completely off balance, upsetting his status quo in a way he will never recover from, but from which he will grow enormously as a human being. And it sets the stakes very high—life or death. The question the audience asks is what is going to happen to Ron? Will he really die in thirty days? And what can he even do to prevent that from happening? Will he, in other words, heed the call to adventure or not?

4. *Doubt, debate, decision* (beginning around page 13–17). This is the story beat in which the debate and decision to act take place. The hero has been called to adventure, been asked to change, but they often have doubts. They are often reluctant to change, because they have grown comfortable with their status quo. Ron Woodruff, in DALLAS BUYERS CLUB, is perfectly comfortable living his life on the edge, burning the candle at both ends. And when the change comes, the protagonist reacts in shock and dismay at the sudden disruption of their status quo. After the catalyst occurs, Ron erupts in anger, defiantly shouting that he is not going to die of AIDS. Not now, not ever. *I got a news flash for all y'all, there ain't nothin' out there that can kill Ron Woodroof in thirty days.*

    Sometimes, like Woodruff, the protagonist is in complete denial that there's a problem that they need to solve at all. They have suddenly and shockingly lost their comfortable place in the world, and like any human being they often experience the five stages of grief and loss, as laid out by Elizabeth Kubler Ross: (1) Denial and isolation; (2) Anger; (3) Bargaining; (4) Depression; (5) Acceptance. In dramatic writing, we don't always need to see all these stages played out in the first act, because we intuitively know they exist. But we do need to see one or more of them illustrated if we are to connect emotionally with the protagonist.

    When their world is turned upside down, the hero at first often completely ignores the problem (total denial) and like Ron Woodruff in DALLAS BUYERS CLUB parties like it's still the old days, which doesn't work out well for Mr. Woodruff. He then isolates himself in the library researching AIDS, until he realizes he most definitely could have contracted it from unprotected sex, which leads to him screaming in anger, then being depressed at this horrible knowledge, and ultimately into acceptance. Only then does he act to solve the problem. Woodruff is a classic example of the **reluctant**

hero who refuses to take on the problem. After the catalyst disrupts his status quo in a big way, he spends the next 15 minutes of the movie trying to prove to himself that what the doctors have just told him cannot be true. He's working through Kubler Ross's five stages, and at the end of this story beat, after having gone from anger, to denial, to grief, he accepts this as his fate and take his first action to attempt to deal with the problem.

Other times the protagonist is so eager to jump in the river and swim for the golden treasure that lies on the other shore that they fail to see all the man-eating crocodiles lurking just below the surface, despite the warnings of others. Indiana Jones is this kind of protagonist, the classic **gung-ho hero**. The minute he hears about the Ark, he's ready to pack his bags and go after it. The voice of doubt comes from Marcus Brody, his friend and colleague. Brody cautions the over eager Jones to think before he rushes off to find the Ark, telling him that this artifact is unlike anything he's gone after before. It's dangerous. Indy laughs off Marcus' concern.

In some stories, the doubt and debate that lead to the hero deciding to leave their status quo world and enter a new world, the antithesis world, is brief. This beat can sometimes be very brief, as in the two or three lines of dialogue in the action thriller BREAKDOWN where Kurt Russell and his wife (Kathleen Quinlan) briefly debate who will go with the trucker to get help when their car breaks down in the remote desert (the catalyst of that story). Brief doubt and debate beats most often occur in **B-movies** like BREAK-DOWN, where characters and settings are more generic, more familiar to audiences, who know the "rules" of the genre, and don't need to be shown extended scenes to get them involved with the characters and the story. The audience for these movies wants to get to the fun stuff quickly.

In films that don't rely as much on specific genre conventions, and instead work to create a unique world populated with original characters, this beat often takes several scenes to get the point across. In LEGALLY BLONDE, for example, which is both a generic comedy and an artfully told tale, it takes several scenes to accomplish this story beat. First, Elle wallows in self-pity after Warner unexpectedly dumps her (the catalyst), then decides to follow her ex-boyfriend to Harvard Law school to win him back, ignoring the doubts of her sorority friends who try to talk her out of this crazy notion. We'll discuss scene construction in more detail in the next chapter, as well as in Part Two. The key thing to remember here is that the point of this beat is to get your hero from the moment their status quo is upset to the moment they enter the new world of the second act, the anti-thesis world, the place where they will have to actually solve their problem or struggle to achieve their goal.

The doubt and debate beat for the reluctant hero, whether it's done in one brief scene or a series of scenes, is the story beat in which the main character momentarily tries to go back to what's comfortable, often as quickly as possible. Only when the protagonist is out of options, when they have lost the debate, does that change, and so this beat often is a refusal of the call to adventure.

When the hero is not a reluctant one at all, when he or she is eager to jump into their adventure, there may be only one scene of doubt as in RAIDERS, or there may be a series of scenes in which others attempt to talk them out of and sometimes even physically stop them from foolishly leaping before they look. This is the case in LEGALLY BLONDE. In both stories, the heroes are eager to heed the call (though Elle certainly takes a moment to grieve), and their closest friends try to caution them about looking before they leap. Indiana Jones and Elle Woods exhibit little reluctance, if any, to leaping into the adventure, and so the doubt and debate must come from the other characters. But it must come if we want the audience to be engaged with the hero's quest.

The doubt is the embodiment of the most basic of dramatic questions: what will happen to the protagonist? Asking this question helps emotionally connect the audience to the hero. It answers the *why should we care* question. For the gung-ho hero like Elle, it's often about realizing they can't listen to all the naysayers around them telling them not do what they so badly want to do. The protagonist must counter all the arguments against taking action, and then they can act to go after what they so badly want, the consequences be damned.

With either type, reluctant hero or gung-ho hero, this beat exists because it reflects once again human nature in the face of adversity or opportunity. When confronted with a radical change to our circumstances, we either refuse to admit we have a problem or we jump headlong into trying to solve it. We either bury our heads in the sand, or dive into the deep end head first. We ignore the call to action, trying to avoid dealing with the problem. We hide under the blankets, ignoring the problem, eating bonbons like Elle, because as the joke goes, denial is the longest river known to man. Or we are subjected to a million reasons why we shouldn't do something, even though we really want to do it.

Ultimately, we can't just sit around and debate with ourselves or others, though, if we want to regain our peaceful, comfortable life, if we want to get that thing we want so badly. In the end, we realize we must do something. The hero has to make the decision to leave the comfort of their status quo thesis world. They will have to put aside doubt, end the debate, and set out to achieve the goal. They act to fulfill their want, in the hope that that this action will result in everything going back to the way it was before the catalyst arrived.

Act Two
Sequence 3

5. *Entering the New World* (beginning around page 25–30). Now that the hero has chosen to leave the comfort of their status quo world to get what they want, the story moves into the second act. Many a second act even begins with a journey of some kind, a trip, a car ride, a plane ride, a walk across a bridge, into the antithesis world, the new world of the second act. Dorothy heads off on the Yellow Brick Road. Indiana Jones hops a plane to Nepal. Elle drives from LA to Boston. All of these are visual metaphors for the dramatic turn the story takes from Act One to Act Two.

The second act can seem a long scary journey for many a screenwriter, and many young writers have gotten lost and given up once they wade into what looks at first like an impenetrable jungle. But with our sixteen beats to help guide us, we as writers can move forward to the fun stuff, the rising action of our script, where most of the great moments in cinema lie. To do so, we once again must call on human psychology to help us. Most people, when confronted with a problem, look for the most obvious solution that pops into their heads. So it should be with the protagonist. Just like they did at the end of the first act when they tried to ignore the problem, or fix it quickly, in this new world of the second act the protagonist will first do the logical, obvious, or easiest thing to get what they want.

In DALLAS BUYERS CLUB, Ron starts his quest by illegally procuring AIDS drugs from the hospital pharmacy, not because it's the right thing to do, or the best thing, but because it's the only thing he can think of to do at the moment. If he doesn't want to die, and he now knows he is dying, he needs to act, and all he knows right now is that he's heard AZT may help. So he goes about getting it in the fastest way possible, from the janitor at the hospital whom he befriends at a strip club (a nice visual symbol of his first act, status quo, thesis world, the world he wishes he could go back to). It's the easiest, quickest, most logical thing for Ron to do, and thus the most believable thing for him to do. In RAIDERS, Indy flies to Nepal in search of Abner Ravenwood who he thinks holds the key to finding the Ark, even though he's told us that he's had a falling out with Abner. Abner is the expert on the Ark, though, so if he wants to find the Ark, that's where he must go first. It's the obvious, logical thing to do.

The problem, as our heroes and heroines quickly find out, is that first attempts to achieve goals always fail. This first logical attempt to achieve the goal, to solve the problem, does not succeed. In DALLAS BUYERS CLUB, Ron's hospital drug scam is quickly busted. In RAIDERS, Indy doesn't find Abner, he finds Marion Ravenwood, Abner's daughter, drinking away her pain over their failed romance from 10 years ago in a bar, and she's pissed to see him. She also lets him know that Abner is dead, which throws a rather large monkey wrench into his attempt to quickly find the Ark.

In LEGALLY BLONDE, Elle goes to Harvard Law school, not because she really wants to be a lawyer, but because that's where her ex-boyfriend Warner has gone, and that's what she thinks she must do if she wants to get him back. The decision seemed like the only possible one left for her to make, so Elle arrives at Harvard to begin her quest, only to learn that Warner has a new girlfriend, Vivian. Problem not solved. Goal not achieved.

The first attempt to achieve the goal fails not just because people are lazy, but because human nature always has us looking for the easy way out. It also fails because the audience wants it to fail. We want to see our heroes earn their rewards, not have them handed over on a silver platter. A thing gotten cheaply and easily is a thing of little value, not something worth fighting to get.

In the narrative world of storytelling, the first attempt at achieving the goal also fails because the protagonist has a flaw, an inner need, that they have not resolved yet. If they succeed here in this beat, they will never confront their own flaw and deal with it, and thus never honestly, believably achieve their goal. The protagonist must earn their success, or the audience won't buy it, and the character won't appreciate it. The hero(ine) is going to have to do better than make an obvious, though logical attempt at achieving their goal if they really want to succeed.

6. *Find Some Allies* (between pages 25 and 45). Having flopped in their first attempt, the protagonist often does the next logical thing, which is, like the drowning man, to look for help. If you can't solve the problem easily by yourself, you look for someone who can at least help you solve it. In this beat, heroes often meet guides, mentors, and sometimes love interests, who they hope can guide them to the promised land.

   In RAIDERS, Indy manages to reconnect with his old flame, Marion Ravenwood, and then with his old friend, the Egyptian digger Sallah, who both offer to help him find the Ark. In DALLAS BUYERS CLUB, Ron makes a connection with Dr. Eve Saks, an honest, caring doctor who he hopes will help him get the medicine he needs, but who will also be key to helping Ron deal with his issues, his flaw, and grow as a person. In THE WIZARD OF OZ, Dorothy recruits three of the most famous allies in all of cinema, all of whom will be crucial in helping her get what she wants.

   Allies, like themes, can appear in beats other than this one. Eve Saks, who will turn out to be an important ally to Ron Woodruff in DALLAS BUYERS CLUB, appears in the catalyst beat. Allies can appear as early as the opening, and even sometimes appear as late as near the end of Act Two, as in LEGALLY BLONDE, when one-time nemesis Prof. Stromwell, who humiliated Elle in the previous beat, becomes an ally near the end of Act Two when she tells Elle not to give up the fight so easily in the beauty salon where Elle has gone to say goodbye to her friend and manicurist, Paulette. Again, flexibility allows for creativity here.

   Many times, the hero's relationships with their allies are depicted in what Snyder calls the **B-Story**. This secondary plot often serves to highlight the theme of the main plot. A love interest or a mentor will often appear to help our hero resolve their inner need, help them deal with their flaw, so the B-Story is often a love story in a movie.

In RAIDERS, the B-story revolves around Indy's romantic relationship with Marion. In LEGALLY BLONDE, a B-Story starts in this beat when Elle meets Emmett sitting on a park bench, after she's been humiliated by Prof. Stromwell, and he gives her advice for handling each of her law professors. The connection between the two is real, and potentially romantic, but whether Elle and Emmett fall in love is not the dramatic question, not the main plot or **A-Story**, because the movie really isn't about Elle finding validation in the love of a man, but about realizing her own self-worth.

Sequence 4

7. *Try A Little Harder* (between page 35/45 and 50/55). With the help of an ally or two that they have recruited, the hero now sets their sights on another attempt to get what they want. This time, often fueled by anger at their first failure, they push a little harder to achieve their goal. Blake Snyder calls this beat **Fun and Games**, and it's a good way to think of it. This is often where big set pieces occur in action movies, or westerns, or musicals.

    In RAIDERS, this beat is illustrated in the Cairo scenes. Indy and Marion leave Nepal and fly to Egypt, where they connect with Sallah and then the real fun and games start, complete with a monkey, poison dates, a mad chase in giant wicker baskets in the bazaar, a sword-wielding thug, and a fiery explosion. The tension rises as the hero begins to really push to solve their problem, to achieve their goal. And the antagonist, the villain, starts pushing back.

    In DALLAS BUYERS CLUB, Ron is thwarted in his first attempt, the illegal procurement of AZT, so he heads to Mexico where he meets defrocked Dr. Vass and learns that AZT is poison. Vass will become a major ally, like Eve and Rayon. Rayon, a cross-dressing homosexual, helps Ron navigate the underground gay world of Dallas. Ron at first treats Rayon with homophobic disdain, because Ron is a bigot. This is his flaw. His inner need is that he must come to learn that everyone, regardless of sexual orientation, is a human being worthy of kindness and compassion.

    In the first act, Ron's narrowminded self-centered view of the world doesn't include being a friend to gay people. But as this B-Story line progresses through the second act, it becomes apparent to Woodruff that Rayon can help him in his quest, and he slowly begins to warm up to Rayon, who like him, is a human being suffering unjustly. If Ron wants to succeed, he needs to try a little harder, and one of the things he must do is to convince Rayon to guide him into the world of gay dance clubs and AIDS support groups, where he can seek answers to help him achieve his goal.

Ron is having a fun time in his attempts to circumvent his own death, but the bad guys have gotten a whiff of him now too. He's stopped in the airport by a FDA agent, who wants to know what all these drugs are that "Father Ron" is bringing into the country. Ron manages to talk his way out of this potentially bad situation, but all the fun and games are going to come to an end very soon when the hero is confronted with a moment that both terrifies him or her, but also clarifies the problem, and the solution, once and for all.

8. *Clarifying the Problem* (somewhere between page 50 and 60). This beat occurs near the half-way point of the movie, the **midpoint** in screenwriting parlance. The midpoint, as everyone from Syd Field to Frank Daniel to Blake Snyder has correctly pointed out, is a turning point in the plot that is just as important as the end of Act One and the end of Act Two. As the hero attempts to achieve their goal, they find the going getting tougher. Part of the reason is because the hero doesn't yet understand the full nature of the problem, they only think they do. It's not until the midpoint, that the problem will be clarified for the hero.

The midpoint, as we said in describing sequence four, often occurs in the **darkest cave**, the place where metaphorically speaking our hero is at their most frightened or vulnerable, but also a place which holds the key in some way to achieving their goal. It is in this darkest cave that the true nature of the hero's problem is often revealed to the hero and the audience. Neither may fully understand the meaning of this revelation, as in the case of THE EMPIRE STRIKES BACK, where neither Luke nor the audience realize that the actual problem that Luke will have to resolve is that Darth Vader is not just a villain, he is Luke's father.

At the beginning of this beat in RAIDERS, Indy's reacting to both the loss of one ally (Marion), and to having figured out that the Nazis are digging for the Ark in the wrong place. The Fun and Games are over. He and Sallah now infiltrate the Nazis' dig site, and Indy uncovers the actual location of the Ark. Under the cover of darkness, they begin digging, and discover the Well of Souls, a giant cavernous pit, long hidden from sight. But this is not just any old pit. It's literally filled with snakes! *Asps. Very deadly!* The opening beat told us that Indy's mortified by snakes, and now he must enter this snake filled pit if he wants to find out where the Ark is hiding. He must literally enter his darkest cave, to face the thing he fears most, which is not the Nazis or Belloq, whom he's fearlessly confronted before, but snakes. So, he takes a deep breath, takes the plunge into the dark cave, and through ingenuity and with Sallah's help he confronts his fear and miraculously finds exactly what he was looking for—the Ark of the Covenant itself. Only by our hero facing his worst fear in the darkest cave, could he have pulled this off.

By entering the darkest cave, our hero should also get clarification of the problem. This clarification of the problem happens in RAIDERS exactly here at the midpoint. Immediately after Indy uncovers and removes the Ark from the Well of Souls, waiting for him outside the darkest cave are a whole lot of Nazis, who gratefully take possession of the Ark. The real problem is now clear. Up to this point in the story, Indy thought his true nemesis was Belloq. The opening scene set this up nicely. But Indy clearly realizes here at the midpoint that it's the Nazis who control Belloq, and they are the real villains, specifically Col. Deitrich and his henchman, SS Commander Toht. They are the ones Indy will have to ultimately defeat if he wants to secure the Ark once and for all. The rest of Act Two will be a series of beats and scenes of Indy vs. the Nazis.

In DALLAS BUYERS CLUB, Ron enters the darkest cave when he follows Rayon into the gay night club. This dark cavernous space is the embodiment of Ron's biggest fear. He is so homophobic he even believed at first that he couldn't possibly have contracted AIDS because to him AIDS was a gay disease. Now in the dimly lit night club, he sees a room full of gay men dancing provocatively, crotch grabbing, and it unnerves him. He's repulsed. Then Rayon tells him that the place is full of potential customers, and he with the most honey will attract the most bees. He should try it sometime. This is something that Ron can comprehend intellectually, and so he tries it out, and has some success. He's starting to become a little less homophobic, and he's warming up to Rayon, but he's not a changed man yet. So, despite learning something valuable (that gay men are human beings just like him and that they can help each other), he insults the next guy who gives him money for drugs. *Fuck off*, he tells a polite young gay man who thanks him after Ron sells him the drugs, and then Ron leaves the club.

As Snyder also illustrates, the midpoint can work one of two ways: "[A] movie's midpoint is either an 'up' where the hero seemingly peaks (though it is a false peak), or a 'down' when the world collapses all around the hero (though it is a false collapse)." The midpoint in RAIDERS is a good illustration of the midpoint as an "up" beat. After all the fun and games and all the *Trying a Little Harder*, Jones actually finds the Ark, outsmarting Belloq and the Nazi's to get it. Things are looking great, but it's only temporary, just a false peak, as we soon see. His achieving of the goal, finding the Ark, is temporary. He hasn't yet "earned the right" to succeed, because he hasn't dealt with his inner need.

We know this because, just before finding the Ark, Indy also found Marion alive. But instead of freeing her and escaping with the woman who loves him, he leaves her tied up so as not to jeopardize his quest. Still obsessed, still arrogant. Bad Indy. Indy's relationship with Marion, which began fully in beat #6, *Finding Some Allies*, is the B-story plot, and this **subplot** must be resolved before the main plot can be fully resolved. We saw the first hint of this when Indy asks Marcus Brody, eyes down and looking away, if he thinks Marion will be in Nepal, where he is going to seek out Abner Ravenwood, in the debate beat. Marion represents Jones' inner need, his flaw. He treats her callously, despite her loving him. He is what Abner said he was, "a bum". Even though Indy's thrilled to find her alive, he immediately backslides and leaves her in jeopardy. Clearly Indy's still got some growing to do. His suffering will have to grow worse before he learns his lesson fully and changes as a person for the better.

The perfect illustration of the midpoint as a down beat occurs in LEGALLY BLONDE. Elle has made some real headway in getting Warner to see her as more than just a blonde, but she hasn't yet come to realize, despite plenty of signs before this, that Warner is not worth the effort she's putting into regaining him, and that that might not be what she really needs (to get Warner back) to be successful as a woman, to find her own power as a woman. This realization happens for Elle when Vivian, Warner's new girlfriend, invites Elle to what Elle mistakenly believes is a costume party.

This party turns out to be Elle's darkest cave. Elle arrives dressed in a Playboy bunny suit, thinking her obvious physical charms will impress Warner, but the party turns out to not really be a costume party at all, and she ends up looking like a complete fool in front of all her Harvard Law School peers. Having confronted her worst fear (looking like a dumb blonde), she doesn't give up easily. Instead of running away immediately in red-faced embarrassment, Elle confronts Warner directly, makes another attempt to impress him by telling him that she intends to apply for Professor Callahan's prestigious law internship. But instead of being impressed, Warner laughs at her and tells her that she is wasting her time, a girl like her will never get that internship. At that moment, Elle realizes that she will never be "good enough" for Warner, that she will never win him back. And here, in her encounter in the darkest cave at the midpoint, she finds the motivation to prove herself worthy of not Warner, but of success as a law student, on her own merits.

Elle has realized that self-empowerment is the key to happiness, she has clarified her problem, what she really needs to achieve her goal, but she's not yet ready to accept that, because it means giving up on Warner. She's not ready to put that valuable knowledge into action, not entirely. She has been shown the answer to her problem (forget Warner and concentrate on herself), been shown the way to resolve her inner need (believing that only by getting married can a woman find true happiness). The key to achieving her goal has been revealed. But she isn't yet going to be able to implement that solution right away. Not yet, and not so easily. For that to happen, things will have to get worse, before they get better, for the heroine. The forces of evil will make sure of that.

Sequence 5

9. *The Forces of Antagonism Respond* (beginning around page 55–60). At this point, the hero through his or her efforts to achieve their goals, has drawn the full attention of the villain. In DIE HARD, this is the point where Alan Rickman realizes he is dealing with Bruce Willis, and that he must kill Bruce to get what he wants. In many films, the villain doesn't even acknowledge the hero until this beat, and sometimes they don't even appear until this beat, or beat #8 just before this. But now the antagonist has been riled up, and they will come out of the shadows and respond with force. This response leads to an escalation of the conflict between protagonist and antagonist.

In DALLAS BUYERS CLUB, Ron's apparent success at beating AIDS takes a startling downturn. First, he reacts badly to the drug he brought in from Japan which sends him to the hospital, then the FDA agent Barkley shows up at the hospital to tell him he's seized all his drugs. They are going to shut down his whole operation. *"Here this. I will bust you, I will take your drugs and I will burn them. You're done."* Woodruff isn't going down without a fight though. He taunts agent Barkley and Dr. Sevard. *You said I'd be dead in thirty days, and howdyfuckindoody, it's a year later, and look who's still here.* The battle between hero and villain is now fully engaged.

Similarly, in LEGALLY BLONDE, after Elle has proven herself worthy to Warner, she draws the attention of Prof. Callahan. Callahan will turn out to be the real villain. Callahan draws Elle into his inner circle, by giving her an internship at his firm, much to Warner's and Vivian's shock, and the audience thinks it's because Callahan believes she's a good lawyer. But we know she's just a first-year law student still trying to figure things out. The audience doesn't need to know yet that Callahan is a villain, that surprise will be saved for a later beat. But the story has taken a clear turn, and from now until the end of the story, the plot will focus around Elle's internship with Callahan's firm.

This beat comprises a series of back and forth scenes that show the confrontation between hero and villain. Like a boxing match, the two begin to go toe to toe, each one responding to the other's actions—first the villain lands a haymaker, then the protagonist swings back. In LEGALLY BLONDE, Elle responds to Warner telling her no one is taking her seriously at Harvard by landing a coveted internship at Callahan's firm. She then begins to prove her worthiness by working diligently to figure out how a young woman accused of murder is innocent.

In RAIDERS, the true villains, the Nazis, respond to Indy's "false peak" success by taking the Ark right back, tossing Marion into the snake pit with him, and then sealing the opening so they cannot ever hope to escape. Now stuck alone with Marion in a pit filled with snakes (the literal manifestation of both inner need and his ultimate fear), Indy is forced to respond to the antagonist's actions. He works furiously to escape the pit, and does so, only to see the Nazi's readying to leave with the Ark. This sets up a wild back and forth series of confrontational scenes, that ultimately lead to Indy momentarily re-capturing the Ark.

10. *The Hero Retreats* (around page 60–70). Our hero, who's just had the full forces of evil unleashed on them directly, almost always does the smart thing, the human thing, and retreats. In RAIDERS, with the Ark in his possession, Indy flees for America on the steam ship with Marion after his multiple tussles with the Nazis in Egypt. Indy has taken a beating getting the relic back, and he's not interested in another confrontation with the Nazis. He's exhausted. He just wants to hide out on this ship until he's back home, in his thesis world, comfortable, safe and sound. But of course, retreating only buys the protagonist a temporary retrieve, as the antagonist has not yet been defeated.

    From a dramatic, structural view point, the hero is not ready yet to defeat the villain because he or she hasn't yet resolved his or her inner need. The resolution of their inner need, the overcoming of their main character flaw, usually is a wrapping up of the B-Story. In RAIDERS, screenwriter Lawrence Kasdan has been laying the breadcrumb trail of the B-story, where most inner needs are resolved, in Indy's relationship with Marion. Indy has resisted changing, resisted Marion, up until now, despite his strong feelings for her. Bruised and bloodied by his recent confrontation with the forces of the antagonist, Marion attempts to clean up his wounds, and he resists again, firmly telling her he doesn't need any help, doesn't need a nurse. He is not yet ready to be vulnerable with her, to show his softer side. She knows better. And after a moment or two of conflict, he finally seems to figure it out too, allowing her to kiss away his aches and pains. The two of them wake up in bed together the next morning, clearly having resolved their "issues". Indy is no longer the callous cad, he's changed. He's grown. Indy has overcome his fear of genuine intimacy with Marion. But all will not remain well, because retreating is just hiding from the inevitable confrontation, the climax, that lies at the heart of every narrative story.

    In DALLAS BUYERS CLUB, now that the real villain is clear, the battle continues in a new vein. Woodruff thought he was fighting AIDS, but the real problem is the government bureaucracy that is blocking AIDS drugs from reaching patients who need them. Ron fights back by convincing all of Dr. Sevard's AZT trial patients to quit the FDA approved test. The battle lines are clearly drawn. From now until the end of the story, it will be Ron against the government that will be the focus of the plot. In DALLAS BUYERS CLUB, the B-story continues as Ron upholds Rayon's "honor" at the grocery store.

Sequence 6

11. *Things Look So Bleak...* (between pages 70 and 90). There's nowhere for the hero to hide in a story, nowhere to retreat, at least not for long, because the villain now knows the hero is a real threat. For example, in THE EMPIRE STRIKES BACK, Darth Vader feels Luke getting stronger under Yoda's tutelage. Vader senses Luke is coming for him, and that can't be allowed. Luke must either be turned or destroyed, otherwise he will destroy Vader. What will happen, what the outcome of this struggle will be, we will unveil as writers when the story reaches its climax. But first, we must make things worse for our hero.

In RAIDERS, the Nazi's interrupt Jones' burgeoning tryst with Marion on the steam ship when they show up in a U-boat and seize the Ark, and take Marion for good measure. The protagonist is back to square one, and now he's alone. There's no one to help him, no Sallah, no Marion, no one. If he's going to achieve his goal of retrieving the Ark, he's going to have to do it all by himself. Indy will have to act again, or lose both the Ark and Marion. It's at this moment that the B-Story of Indy and Marion gets tied directly to the main plot, the search for the Ark. And the two plotlines will remain connected until the climax.

In LEGALLY BLONDE, Callahan now finally reveals himself in this beat to be the ultimate villain. Up until this beat Elle, and the audience, have assumed Warner was the villain, then Vivian, then Prof. Stromwell. But because the theme of the film is female empowerment, it would undercut the movie if Vivian or Stromwell were the villain. The villain should be a man, and the ultimate "man-villain", the symbol of the corrupt patriarchal society, will turn out to be Callahan. He represents the exact antithesis to Elle's thesis world. In her sorority life (the status quo of her thesis world), she is the power in charge, and her sorority sisters love and support her. It's a genuine sisterhood, not a dictatorship. But the law, especially Harvard Law, is a boys' club ruled by powerful men, and women like Elle are only good for one thing, and it's not to be interns. Callahan makes his move here, literally, and Elle is shocked and devastated. She walks out of his office crushed by his unwanted sexual advance. She believes she will never be taken seriously as a lawyer or a person as long as men are in charge. Things look so bleak for our heroine, we literally feel as if her dream is dead.

In DALLAS BUYERS CLUB, the FDA shuts down Ron's buyers' club and confiscates all his drugs. No one will sell him the AIDS drugs he needs, and the IRS is now after him too. Things can't get worse. He is now mortally threatened. It looks like the villain is going to win, and our hero is going to be vanquished. If the screenwriter has done his job, the audience will fear the worst is about to happen, and there's nothing anyone can do about it.

12. *Metaphorically Dead* (occurs somewhere around page 75–90). Once things have gone totally south for the protagonist, the only place more down than bleak is dead. Not literally dead, but most often metaphorically. Snyder calls this moment "the whiff of death", but you can't smell anything in a movie, so it's usually a visual metaphor of death that we see, a "vision of death". This moment is often brief, but it's very powerful. We not only feel like all is lost, and that our hero will never succeed, but we also feel for a moment that they are dead.

In LEGALLY BLONDE, Elle walks out of Callahan's office, after having been stunned by his sexual proposition, into a darkened elevator, and there she sees her reflection mirrored in the closing door. It's like we've literally put the lid on her casket, and she's now enveloped in darkness. It's as if she, and the audience, are looking at a ghost of the now dearly departed young lady. At this point the villain appears to have cornered the hero, and the hero feels utterly alone, defeated. They feel dead. To cement this feeling even further, Elle walks past Emmett, who we clearly know likes her, and brushes him off despite his attempt to get her to stay, and not quit and go back to Los Angeles. She feels defeated, and the audience feels like her quest has failed. She's completely alone now. If she's going to achieve her goal of finding validation, she's going to have to do it alone

In DALLAS BUYERS CLUB, we get the "whiff of death" at first not from Ron, but from Rayon, who looks in the mirror and tells God that when he sees Him, he wants to look pretty, like an angel. We sense clearly that Rayon is dying. The B-Story between Ron and Rayon now reaches its own climax. Earlier, Ron exhibited some genuine compassion, helping a suffering Rayon ease his pain with a syringe full of narcotics. Now in this beat, when Rayon responds with kindness of his own by giving Ron the money to keep his business afloat, Ron finally embraces him, accepting Rayon for who he is, with genuine love and appreciation. Ron, the ultimate cowboy homophobe, has become Ron the compassionate caregiver.

In LEGALLY BLONDE, it's Prof. Stromwell, in a nice **twist**, who helps Elle resolve her inner need and learn that she doesn't need a husband to validate herself as a woman. Elle first must confront and resolve her own inner need, self-worth. This happens right after she has appeared to be metaphorically dead. As Elle shares her darkest moment in a tearful goodbye with her ally Paulette, the manicurist, it appears to the audience that Ms. Woods has thrown in the towel and given up her quest. But then Stromwell reveals herself (literally, popping up from under a hair dryer) as an ally, telling Elle that if she gives up now, she's not the girl the professor thought she was. Now is not the time to quit the fight, now is the time to put the lesson she's learned to use. She must stand up for herself.

Similarly, in RAIDERS before the main plot is resolved, before Indy achieves his goal, before the climax of the story, he and the audience must experience the bleakest moment of the story, in which the hero will not only encounter apparent defeat at the hands of the villain, but he will also appear to be dead. When the Nazis show up in the U-boat and seize the tramp steamer, Indy retreats again. He watches as they take back the Ark and grab Marion. The Colonel wants Indy too, but the ship Captain tells *herr colonel* that Indy is already dead. He killed him. For a moment, we laugh, because we just saw Indy hiding in the smoke stack, but when the German's leave, the crew go in search of Indy, and he's nowhere to be found. Suddenly the rug has been pulled out from under us. For a moment, we think that somehow, Indiana Jones just might be dead. He's certainly nowhere among the living on the steam ship. Of course, in a moment he will pop up on top of the U-boat, having jumped ship, and everyone, audience and crew applaud Indy's miraculous return from the dead.

Before Elle or Indy can achieve their goals, fulfill their wants, learn that true happiness does not lie in the arms of Warner, or in getting the Ark, we need to see that they have grown as human beings, otherwise, the victory won't feel as sweet, it won't feel rightly and justly earned. So, the Stromwell and Marion B-Stories must reach a climax first, before Elle and Indy get what they want. The climax of the B-Story line shows us that the protagonist is not finished, not dead, they have been reborn, and they are ready now for the final confrontation with the antagonist. The hero may have learned their lesson, but he or she hasn't yet achieved the goal. That will require something more, something heroic, to achieve. And to find that heroism within, the protagonist had to change by being pushed to the brink of defeat, to a metaphorical death.

Act Three
Sequence 7

13. *Having Learned the Lesson* (beginning around page 75–90). The climax of the story is nearing, but before the protagonist can fairly, squarely, and believably achieve their goal, they must show us that they have not only learned their lesson, but also that they have integrated that knowledge into their very characters. In short, they must show us that they have changed completely.

    In DALLAS BUYERS CLUB, to show the audience that the homophobic cowboy that Ron was at the beginning of the story is no longer who he is now, to show us he's really, truly changed, that he really has resolved his flaw, and dealt with his inner need, and deserves to succeed, Ron must show us that he is no longer the homophobe he was at the start, he has grown and changed. To cement this point, following his embrace of Rayon for giving him money to keep the business afloat, Woodruff tells his secretary to sell his beloved Cadillac to make sure everyone who wants his help gets it, whether they can afford it or not.

    As mentioned, the lesson is often learned through the B-story relationships the protagonist has had with his or her allies. The resolution of the B-stories therefore must come before the main plot in the story is resolved in the climax of the movie because it's in that B-story resolution that the writer shows the audience that our hero(ine) has learned his or her lesson, and can now rightfully achieve their goal.

14. *Once More into the Breach* (between pages 80 and 100). At this point, there's nothing left for our hero to learn or do but to confront the villain, with all the knowledge the hero has gained on his or her journey, one last time. The hero has to give it everything they have if they want to succeed. They must directly confront the villain in order to achieve the goal they have wanted so badly and have had such a hard time getting. As Henry V said as he led his army into battle against the French one last time to save England, the hero must go *once more unto the breach* to get what they want.

    At this point in the story, things may occur very quickly, often in real time. In this beat, the story has picked up pace, gained so much momentum, that the action has risen to a point where it cannot realistically go any higher. We're about to reach the climactic moment in the protagonist's struggle to achieve their goal. This act, beginning with this beat, often occurs in a place that is not the antithesis world of the second act. We're in the synthesis world now, where the conflict is nearing resolution, so in many a movie, this part of the story occurs in a new location.

In LEGALLY BLONDE, Elle is appointed the new lawyer for the young aerobics instructor on trial for murder. Now she will have one last opportunity to prove, not just to the outside world but to herself, that she is worthy, that she has value as a woman, regardless of whether she has a man in her life or not.

In RAIDERS, Indy leaves the antithesis world of the second act (Nepal and Egypt) and enters, reborn into a new world. He miraculously follows the German submarine to a U-boat base in a cave on a Greek island. Here, he puts on the uniform of a Nazi soldier, and using his wits and his stealth goes after the forces of evil, Belloq, the Colonel, and SS man Toht, forcing one final face-off for possession of the Ark.

In DALLAS BUYERS CLUB, Ron now furious at the death of Rayon, goes after Dr. Sevard and then the FDA, the CDC, and the big drug companies in a no holds barred attack on these antagonists. He tells Sevard's patients that Sevard is not a doctor but a killer, and then he tells everyone at a large CDC/FDA gathering that they are nothing but experimental guinea pigs for the big drug companies, who are peddling poison to sick people just to make a buck. Woodruff, like Elle and Indy, is about to fight his final battle with the forces of antagonism.

Sequence 8

15. *The Final Confrontation and Climax* (somewhere in pages 85–110). All that's left now is the climax, the final confrontation between protagonist and antagonist, the final battle between hero and villain. If the hero has learned their lesson, if they deserve to succeed, they almost always do. If they haven't, they will fail, and we will have a **classic tragedy** in the mold of Shakespeare's *Hamlet* on our hands. That's because if the hero does learn their lesson and then doesn't succeed, or if they succeed without having learned anything, without having grown and changed, the audience will be furious. Their moment of **catharsis**, to go all the way back to Aristotle and the Greeks, will have been withheld from them, and no audience likes that.

If they haven't learned their lesson, or like Hamlet learned it too late, if they have not dealt finally and convincingly with their main character flaw, and so resolved their inner need, the protagonist should fail, because again that is what the audience will want. The audience will sense that the protagonist doesn't deserve to be rewarded, because they haven't changed and grown, and they will be angry if they are rewarded despite that.

In LEGALLY BLONDE, Elle takes everything she's learned in law school, and applies the lesson in self-confidence she's gained on her quest to courageously and cleverly get her innocent client off the hook for murder. In RAIDERS, Indy has learned that Marion is more important than the Ark, that love is more important than treasure. He gives up the Ark to the Nazis rather than blow it, and Marion, to smithereens with a bazooka. He then pleads with Marion not to look at the Ark as the Nazi's open it, and this act of love is what saves the two of them from the avenging angel of death that is released and destroys Belloq and all the evil Nazis.

In DALLAS BUYERS CLUB, Ron takes the lesson he's learned, that we're all human beings regardless of sexual orientation who deserve care and compassion, and puts it selflessly to use by giving away club memberships (and thus lifesaving AIDS drugs) to anyone who wants them. Then he takes on the government in one last battle, and even though he doesn't win his battle with the FDA or his fight against AIDS, he has become a truly decent human being through the struggle. This triumph far outweighs his own mortality.

16. *The Takeaway* (the final page or two of the script). In many ways, the final scene is just like the opening scene, and often it's a mirror reverse of it. The final scene, the resolution if you prefer, shows the audience what things are like for the main character now that they have achieved their goal. It shows the audience what the new status quo is, what the synthesis of thesis world and antithesis world looks like through the eyes of the protagonist. There's often a takeaway as well, sometimes a scene or a moment, sometimes just an image or a single line or two, that sums everything up for the audience. Wrapping everything up like this (in the *denouement* as the French call it), along with the theme stated early on which helped to frame and set up everything, answers the dramatic question or thematic premise.

In the takeaway scene of LEGALLY BLONDE, we see Elle two years later graduating law school first in her class. She gives a commencement speech that recaps her amazing journey, and then gets a standing ovation from her peers. And just to put a little ribbon on things, in a little sidebar we find out she's now happily engaged to Emmett. In the takeaway scene of RAIDERS, we see Indy and Marion leave the Ark in the hands of the government, "someplace safe" where no one will ever find it. They walk away together, arm in arm, to get a drink and begin the rest of their lives. In DALLAS BUYERS CLUB, when Ron returns to Dallas, even though he's lost this latest court battle, he is met with a standing ovation by those he has fought so hard to help. As the film ends, we're told the FDA later allowed Woodruff to take peptide T for personal use and that he died of AIDS in 1992, seven years later than his doctors initially said he would.

At this point, the only thing left to write in the screenplay are the last two words of every script: *THE END.*

Example: *Get Out*

1. *Opening Scene.* An African-American man walks around an affluent neighborhood lost, and a bit nervous. He talks to someone on a cellphone and tells them he "sticks out like a sore thumb" in this creepy white suburban enclave. A white car then begins to follow him. Feeling uncomfortable, the man decides to leave the area, but it's too late—the driver of the white car, wearing a medieval knight's helmet, overpowers the man, tosses him in the trunk of the car, and drives off.

2. *The Status Quo.* Chris Washington, a talented African-American photographer is packing, when his girlfriend, Rose Armitage, shows up with some pastries. Chris is feeling a bit nervous because he and Rose are about to head to her parents' house in the country for the weekend. He's nervous because Rose has never told her parents that Chris is black. Rose assures Chris that her parents are liberal and would have voted for Obama for a third presidential term if he had run. She tells Chris he has nothing to worry about.

3. *The Catalyst.* As they drive upstate, Chris calls his buddy Rod and asks him to watch his dog. Rod tells him to be careful because a black man should never go to a white girlfriend's parents' house or "something bad will come." Chris laughs it off and hangs up, and as soon as he does, Rose hits a deer as it darts across the road. Freaked out, Chris leaves the car to check on the

animal. He follows its plaintive moans into the woods, and when he spots it, he seems almost paralyzed by the awful sight of the dying animal.

4. *Doubt, debate and decision.* Badly shaken, Chris is leaning against the SUV, when a white police officer arrives on the scene and asks Rose and Chris about the accident. The officer asks to see Chris's ID. Rose snaps at the officer, tells him she was driving, not Chris, and accuses the white officer of basically profiling Chris because he's black. The officer denies it, telling her he's just following standard operating procedure. Chris shows the officer his license, and tells Rose to let it go.

   They arrive at Rose's parents' house, an affluent country mansion, and Chris meets the Armitages. Rose's parents, Dean and Missy, seem nice enough, but Chris becomes a little unsettled again when he sees the Armitage's have two African-Americans working for them: Georgina the maid and Walter the groundskeeper. Mr. Armitage assures Chris it's not how it looks. He kept Georgina and Walter employed with the family after his parents died because he felt it was the right thing to do.

   Later, on the patio, Missy notices that Chris is fidgeting. She figures out quickly that he's a smoker who's having nicotine withdrawals. Missy turns out to be a hypnotherapist, and she offers to hypnotize Chris to cure him of his nasty habit. Dean tells Chris his wife hypnotized him, and he stopped smoking cold turkey. Chris declines Missy's offer, a little unsettled about somebody poking around in his head.

   At dinner that night, Chris meets Rose's brother, who questions Chris about his athleticism in a rather overtly racist way. Chris again shrugs off the slight. Later alone with Chris, Rose apologizes to Chris, surprised her family acted so stereotypically racist. In so many words, Chris says, I told you so.

5. *Entering the New World.* Later that night he wakes up, jonesing for a cigarette. He heads outside for a smoke and sees Walter running straight at him in a mad sprint—and then veering off suddenly. Then through the window, he sees Georgina looking at herself in the mirror in an odd way. Something very strange is going on here. On his way back in, he runs into Missy, who insists he join her in the study.

   She's upset that Chris is a smoker and wants to help him quit. She has a cup of tea, gently stirring it with a spoon. Missy starts asking questions about

Chris' past. We learn that when he was 11, at home watching TV, his mother was struck by a hit-and-run driver and left dying in the road. Chris did nothing when she failed to come home on time, and the guilt has been with him ever since. (This is why he was so upset when they hit the deer with the car earlier.) Missy continues stirring the spoon in the tea cup, and the effect is irresistible. Just like that, Chris is hypnotized. He "falls" into "the sunken place," a dark void somewhere in Chris' mind where he can only see what's happening out of a tiny rectangular window (that resembles a TV screen). He is powerless to do anything.

Chris wakes up the next morning again unsettled. He tells Rose that he thinks her mom hypnotized him. Rose then notices a line of black cars, like a funeral procession, rolling up the driveway. We heard earlier that she had forgotten that this weekend was her family's traditional annual party for the locals. Chris watches from the window as middle-aged white people emerge from the cars.

6. *Find Some Allies...* Chris does his best to mingle at the party (looking for allies), but encounters subtle racism everywhere he turns. He then meets Jim Hudson, a successful, but blind gallery owner, who seems to share Chris's dim view of all the people in attendance. He tells Chris he wishes he had his "eye", and offers him a gallery showing. Chris is grateful.

    Then Chris, who's been taking photos at the party, spots Logan King, a fellow young black man who appears to have assimilated well with his white neighbors. Maybe too well. Chris talks to Logan, but gets a weird vibe from him.

    (Both Hudson and Logan come across as possible allies, but in great twists Hudson later turns out to be in cahoots with the villain, and Logan turns out be under the villain's control).

    Chris goes up to his room and calls his ally Rod. Chris tells him that Missy may have hypnotized him last night and that things are very weird here. Rod, who is a TSA officer, has a conspiratorial side and tells Chris what he thinks is going on—black people are being hypnotized and turned into "sex slaves." Chris again shrugs this off as crazy talk.

7. *Try Again, But Harder This Time.* Georgina appears in the doorway. She explains that she was dusting around the room and may have accidentally unplugged Chris' phone. When Chris tries to speak with Georgina, she again

acts very bizarre, as if she's struggling with something deep inside her. Chris takes his phone and goes back to rejoins the party.

He tries to mingle again, but then one of the guests asks Chris about what the "black experience" is like. Uncomfortable with the question, Chris turns to Logan and asks him to field that question. As Logan fumbles around for an explanation, Chris snaps a picture of him with his cellphone.

8. *Clarify the Problem.* The flash on Chris's cellphone accidentally goes off as he takes the photo, and Logan immediately freezes, as if he's gone into a trance. Then he seems to wake up, and he rushes at Chris, his nose bleeding, and tells him to "Get out!" Chris is stunned by the reaction, and doesn't understand what's going on exactly, but he feels like for a moment, he knew who Logan was.

9. *The Forces of Antagonism Respond.* Several guests "escort" Logan into the house, and take him away to Missy's study. Missy seemingly "reboots" Logan, who returns and apologizes for his "overreaction", then takes his leave of the party.

10. *The Hero Retreats.* Chris is now totally and completely unsettled by the day's events. He retreats to a quiet place by the lake where Rose finds him. He explains everything that he's experienced so far, and tells her that he wants to go home immediately. Rose is taken aback at first, but Chris is determined. He's leaving with or without his girlfriend. She then agrees to go with him.

11. *Things Look Bleak.* The party ends. Alone, Chris texts the photo he took of Logan to Rod. Rod quickly calls him back right away and tells Chris that "Logan" is really Andre Hayworth (the man who was abducted in the opening scene). Chris begins to panic, and tells Rose to pack, they're leaving now. As she heads off to get ready to leave, Chris spots a closet door that's open. He peeks inside and finds a shoebox filled with photos of Rose in romantic shots with other black people including Walter, Andre, and even Georgina. Chris gets frantic.

Rose shows up. Chris says they need to leave, right now. But she can't find the car keys. The Armitage family meet them in the foyer, "sad" to see them leaving. Everything takes on a sinister edge, as Rose admits she can't give Chris the keys—because they're not leaving. Chris tries to jet out the door, but Rose's brother Jeremy grabs him and they start to wrestle. Missy then taps her tea cup with a spoon, and Chris collapses like a robot who's been turned off.

12. *Metaphorically Dead.* Jeremy and Dean carry Chris down into the basement. He wakes up and finds he's been bound to a chair. Above his head is the stuffed head of a deer. The television snaps on and he sees Jim Hudson, the blind art dealer. Hudson tells Chris he can answer any questions Chris has. Chris finds out that Hudson is going to have his brain implanted in the "superior" body of Chris. This way, he can basically live forever. The Armitage family has been doing this for a generation now. It's 21st century "mind" slavery. Missy's hypnotism was simply a way to prepare Chris's mind for the surgery. Chris freaks out. He is trapped, all hope is gone. When the spoon and tea cup come on the TV set, he panics, but it's no use. He's out like a light again, basically dead.

13. *Once More into the Breach.* Chris wakes again, so worried he's going to literally lose his mind that his fingers tear open the upholstery of the chair he's tied to. Stuffing comes spilling out. He manages to use the stuffing to seal his ears against being hypnotized again. Jeremy shows up in hospital scrubs to retrieve Chris for his brain surgery, thinking Chris is still hypnotized, and Chris bashes him over the head with a bocce ball, apparently killing him.

    Chris flees the sunken room, grabbing the stuffed deer head and impaling Dean with the antlers. Chris runs upstairs, where he confronts Missy. She tries to hypnotize him again with the tea cup and spoon but Chris smashes the cup, then dispatches Missy with a letter opener.

    As Chris makes a run for it, Jeremy turns up again—like a horror movie killer who won't die—and grapples with Chris at the front door, putting him in a headlock. But Chris outwits him, and kills him, this time for good.

14. *Having Learned the Lesson.* Finally outside, Chris jumps into Jeremy's white sports car. He spots a knight's helmet in the passenger seat. Jeremy was the one who must've kidnapped Andre Hayworth in the opening. Chris zooms away from the house, but then Georgina suddenly appears in the headlights. He hits her head on. For a moment, he thinks about leaving her to die. Then, he overcomes his fear, resolving his inner need (the guilt over doing nothing when his mom lay dying in the street) and stops the car and climbs out. This

time he's going to do something after a hit-and-run (something he didn't do for the deer). He helps Georgina into the car. Georgina however turns out be "controlled" by Grandma Armitage, and she attacks Chris. They struggle and the car goes off the road and hits a tree, killing Grandma.

15. *The Final Confrontation.* Chris climbs out of the wrecked car as Rose shows up with a hunting rifle. She fires at Chris, who escapes, only to be chased down by Walter (who's under the spell of Grandpa Armitage). Chris pulls out his smartphone and takes a photo of Walter using the flash, hoping to wake Walter. Rose shows up, ready to shoot Chris, but in an apparent twist, Walter tells her to give him the rifle, he'll do it. When she does, he turns the gun on her, blasting a hole in her stomach. Then, in a twist on the twist, Walter turns the rifle on himself, fires, and thus ends his mental slavery forever.

    As Rose lays dying in the road, Chris moves to finish her off. As he is strangling her, Rose smiles as she sees red and blue lights flash and we hear a siren sounding. It doesn't look good for Chris, a black man, on top of a white woman in the middle of the road, especially because he got so much trouble from the police officer earlier. But it turns out that it's not a cop who's shown up, it's Rod in his TSA car. Chris leaves Rose to die in the street, gets in the car with Rod, and they drive off.

16. *The Takeaway.* In the car, Chris asks Rod how he was able to find him. "I'm T-S-motherfucking-A," Rod says. "We handle shit. That's what we do. Consider this situation fucking handled." Chris and Rod drive away, Chris having survived the ordeal, wiser for the struggle, and with his body and mind still intact. He got out.

EXERCISES

Exercise 1: Break down one of the following movies into 16 story beats.

Aliens
Casablanca
Die Hard
Moonlight
Nightcrawler
True Romance
When Harry Met Sally

Exercise 2: Take the 8 sequences you created for your script in Chapter Four and expand them into 16 story beats.

FURTHER READING:

Save the Cat! by Blake Snyder

Turning 16 Beats Into 40 Scenes

The next step in the process of structuring your screenplay involves moving from 16 story beats to 40 scenes. The question you're probably asking yourself is, *why do I need 40 scenes exactly? Why not 30 or 60 or any other number I choose?* The answer, of course, is that a screenplay should have as many scenes as are necessary to tell the story. In actual practice, the number of scenes in a script varies because every story is different, or at least should be. Certain types of movies, certain genres of films, may have a very similar number of scenes, but there is no exact number a screenplay *must* have. Dialogue driven movies tend to have longer scenes, so there are fewer scenes in these scripts. Action driven movies tend to have shorter scenes, and thus more scenes in total in a full screenplay. Although there is no single fixed number of scenes that a movie requires, the average 110-page script usually has between 40 and 60 scenes. Most scenes are one to three pages long, though scenes can range from one brief line of description in length to several pages long.

The length of your scenes is of little importance right now, but it is very helpful in understanding screenwriting as a process to choose a specific number of scenes, and there is some logic to setting the number at forty. Remember that a movie has three acts, and the second act is roughly twice as long as the first and third acts. The second act also has a natural turning point in the middle (in the *Clarifying the Problem* story beat, sometimes occurring in the darkest cave). If we choose forty as our number of scenes, that gives us a nice, reasonable number of 10 scenes for Act One, 20 scenes for Act Two (10 before the midpoint and 10 after), and 10 scenes for Act Three, for a total number of 40 scenes. In addition, if each of the 16 story beats in our structure takes two scenes to write, that would mean you need 32 scenes total for the whole script. If each beat takes three scenes that would result in 48 total scenes in a script. Splitting the difference, again we get 40 scenes.

If you need more convincing, script structure guru Blake Snyder used 40 scenes as well. Ultimately, you can choose any number of scenes you like for your story, but for clarity and simplicity, and to help better understand the process of screenwriting, we're going to use 40 scenes. Whatever the justification, 40 scenes are a good number to focus on. Once you've gone through this process a few times, you'll choose whatever number of scenes works best for your story. At this point, 40 scenes give you as a writer the necessary flexibility in choosing the number of scenes you need for each story beat. It lets you start to feel *creative*, and so your individual creativity can be put to work now and through the rest of the screenwriting process (new wine in old bottles).

NOTECARDS AND CORKBOARDS

So how do we go from 16 story beats to 40 scenes when laying out the structure of a script? In crafting a screenplay, in moving from structuring it to writing it, writers must start to think in terms of scenes as the basic building blocks of their script. Most of us need some way to help us visualize these building blocks and how they fit together, and over the years in Hollywood a simple method has developed for doing that. This method involves using notecards and corkboards. Each scene in your script is briefly described on a single notecard. As you create notecards you arrange them with stick pins on a corkboard (or tape them on a wall if you don't want to bother with the corkboard).

The notecards can be arranged in a variety of ways. Blake Snyder suggests using 4 horizontal rows, with 10 scenes per row: 10 in row 1 for Act One, 10 in row 2 for the scenes of Act Two up to the midpoint, 10 in row three for Act Two from the midpoint to end of the act, and 10 in row 4 for the scenes in Act Three. I've seen writers use three vertical columns, one for each act. Some people like to color code their notecards, using a different color for each act. Whatever arrangement you choose, the notecards should include the following basic information to describe the scene:

1. Whether the scene is an interior or exterior scene (**INT.** or **EXT.**)
2. Where the scene takes place
3. Whether it's a **DAY** scene or a **NIGHT** scene
4. A very short description of what happens in the scene.
5. A notation of who the **conflict** is between in the scene
6. A notation about the **polarity** of the scene

The first three pieces of information are fairly self-explanatory. For the fourth bit, the description, focus on what the actual point of the scene is. Characters may talk, or take action, but what matters here is not summarizing that, but instead describing what the heart of the scene is. What is revealed, what happens, that moves the story forward to the next scene? Concentrate on that in this description. The fifth and sixth bits (the conflict and the polarity) will require a bit more thought on your part. When you describe your first scene on a notecard, it will look like this:

INT./EXT. NAME OF LOCATION	- DAY/NIGHT
Description of what happens in this scene	
Conflict **between:**	
Polarity: **Up/Down**	

To figure out 5 and 6, you first need to understand what a **scene** is, and how it functions in a screenplay. The dictionary definition is a start: a scene is *the place where some action or event occurs.* In screenwriting terms, a scene is simply a unit of a story that takes place at a specific location and specific time. If either time or location change, you have a new scene. For example, if the story moves from an exterior location to an interior one, it's a new scene. If it moves from one point in time to a moment that is even a few minutes later, that is also a new scene. It's **the unity of place and time** that defines a scene in screenwriting.

The purpose of a scene is to advance the plot (moving the story along) and to reveal something about the character (traits, flaws, growth). To do either, and you should always try to do both wherever possible, you need to have **conflict** in the scene. That's because every scene can be thought of as a little movie, with its own, beginning, middle, and end. Every scene has a setup, rising action, and climax, though we don't always need to see the setup or the climax. Conflict is what shows audiences who a character is and how they are changing. It is the catalyst for change in every scene. Conversely, if your scene has no conflict in it, you either need to create it, or dump the scene. Otherwise that scene serves no purpose in your story, and you should discard it. We'll discuss these notions in more detail in Part Two, but right now, just think of each scene as a little movie.

Scenes in films also tend to end on an "up" beat or a "down" beat. A high note or a low note. We saw one example of this in the two types of midpoints that are possible (in the beat we're calling *Clarifying the Problem*). We contrasted these different midpoint types in LEGALLY BLONDE (a down beat midpoint) and RAIDERS OF THE LOST ARK (an up beat midpoint). This notion of ending on an up or a down beat is sometimes called **scene polarity**, and ideally it should be present in every scene you write. If there is conflict in a scene, that conflict will need an outcome otherwise the scene isn't complete, it hasn't fulfilled its function in the story. Giving the audience an up or a down helps to keep the audience engaged and interested in the overall outcome.

If two characters are in conflict in a scene, and as we've said there should always be some type of conflict in a scene, then the polarity reflects the outcome with respect to the protagonist (or sometimes an ally of the protagonist). Does the scene end on a high note for the hero, or a low note? An up beat for the hero or a down beat? Some writing gurus, like Robert McKee believe that if one scene ends on a down beat, the next must start on a low note and then finish on an up beat, this way the story builds like a stair case through the rising action to the climax and resolution. In practice this isn't always the case, but in the best scripts you will always find polarity in every scene.

Now, armed with these six elements for our notecards, if we were to create a notecard for the first scene of RAIDERS OF THE LOST ARK, it would look something like this:

EXT.	**SOUTH AMERICAN JUNGLE**	**DAY**
	INDIANA JONES moves through the jungle in search of an ancient temple containing a priceless golden idol. The natives who are with him however may not be entirely trustworthy.	
Conflict between:	Indy and the nervous natives	
Polarity:	Scene starts down as natives are tense, afraid, and ends on an up beat when they find the temple	

It's also a very good idea to include either separately on the corkboard or on each notecard individually a notation for what Act the scene is in (and if you want to get even more detailed, what sequence and what story beat). Color coding notecards, with for example white for Act One, yellow for Act Two, and pink for Act Three, is one simple way to do that. You can also make a simple notation somewhere on the card like A1/S1/B1 (for Act 1, Sequence 1, Beat 1) for example. You should have your **beat sheet** handy so that you can always refer to it as you are laying out your scenes. Let's run through the first act of GET OUT to see what it would look like outlined using notecards.

EXT.	**AFFLUENT WHITE SUBURB**	**NIGHT**
	An African-American man wanders lost and nervous through a white neighborhood, and is kidnapped by a mysterious person wearing a medieval knight's helmet.	
Conflict between:	African-American and knight	
Polarity:	Starts up, ends down	

INT.	**CHRIS'S APARTMENT**	**DAY**
	Chris is nervous about visiting his white girlfriend's family. She gets him to relax by telling him they voted for Obama.	
Conflict between:	Chris and Rose	
Polarity:	Starts down, ends up	

EXT.	TWO LANE HIGHWAY, UPSTATE NY	DAY
	Chris and Rose drive to her parents. On the way he talks to his friend Rod, who tells him to be careful around white folks. She jokes that it's Rod that Chris is really in love with. Then they hit a deer (CATALYST)	
Conflict between:	Chris and Rose; Chris and Rod	
Polarity:	Scene starts up (funny), ends down (scary)	

EXT.	IN THE WOODS	DAY
	Chris wants to look for the deer, but Rose is worried for him. He finds it dying in the woods off the side of the road, and becomes emotionally upset.	
Conflict between:	Chris and Rose; Chris and himself	
Polarity:	Starts down, ends worse	

EXT.	SIDE OF ROAD, NEAR SUV	DAY
	A police officer arrives, and questions Rose, and then asks to see Chris's license. Rose accuses the cop of being racist, as Chris tries to defuse the tension.	
Conflict between:	Rose and cop; Chris and Rose	
Polarity:	Starts down (Rose argues with cop), ends up, when Chris defuses the tension	

EXT.	ARMITAGE ESTATE	DAY
	Chris and Rose arrive, and are warmly greeted by her parents. Dad shows Chris picture of his dad, who lost to Jesse Owens and never got over it. Walter, the creepy black groundskeeper, watches.	
Conflict between:	Chris and Rose's dad ("call me Dean, my man!")	
Polarity:	Starts up, warm greeting, ends down, hint of racism and mystery of Walter watching.	

EXT.	BACKYARD PATIO	DAY
	Dean and Missy interrogate Chris. Find out his mom died in a hit and run when he was 11. And that Chris smokes, which both parents disapprove of. Missy offers to "cure" Chris of his nasty habit through hypnosis. He declines.	
Conflict between:	Dad and Chris; Parents and Rose	
Polarity:	Starts up, with humor, ends down with Georgina arriving, spelling drink.	

INT.	DINING ROOM	DAY
	Chris has dinner with the Armitage family. Jeremy makes racist comments about sports and blacks, but is shut down by Rose and her parents.	
Conflict between:	Jeremy and Chris, Jeremy and family	
Polarity:	Starts up, humor ("toe nail clippings") ends down, Jeremy makes Chris uncomfortable	

INT.	GUEST BEDROOM	NIGHT
	Rose apologizes profusely for her family acting stereotypically "white" and racist. "How are they different than that cop?" Chris says I told you so.	
Conflict between:	Chris and Rose	
Polarity:	Starts down, ends up with them in bed	

INT.	GUEST BEDROOM	NIGHT
	Chris wakes up in the middle of the night, can't sleep, thinking about the dead deer. Heads outside for a cigarette hoping it will relax him.	
Conflict between:	Chris and himself (inner need, unresolved guilt)	
Polarity:	Starts down, ends up (he acts, gets out of bed)	

Notecards are a useful tool to help you visualize the overall structure of your script. They are a tried and true method that screenwriters have used for years. As you play with notecards and use them more often, you'll come up with a style that works best to help you visualize your screenplay's structure.

EXERCISES

Exercise 1: Make notecards for all the scenes in one of the following movies...

Aliens
Casablanca

Die Hard
Moonlight
Raiders of the Lost Ark
The Secret Life of Walter Mitty (2013)
True Romance
When Harry Met Sally
The Wizard of Oz

Exercise 2: Take the 16 story beats you created for your script in Chapter Six and expand them into 40 scenes using notecards.

FURTHER READING:

Save the Cat! Goes to the Movies by Blake Snyder.

PART 2
Writing the Screenplay

Crafting Scenes

Up to this point, we've been focused on structuring a screenplay. The structure you created is the skeleton for what will become a fully fleshed out script, like the frame of a house for a finished home. It's the blueprint for your screenplay, but it's not the finished product. When you start writing scenes, you are beginning to put flesh on the lovely bones you've created so far. You finished creating those bones when you laid out all the scenes you needed for your movie on notecards. Each notecard, as in the example below from GET OUT, is the blueprint for an individual scene of your script. This is your starting point.

EXT.	AFFLUENT WHITE SUBURB	NIGHT
	An African-American man, lost and nervous, is kidnapped by a mysterious person wearing a medieval knight's helmet.	
Conflict between:	African-American man and knight	
Polarity:	Starts up, ends down	

The next step in the process is to begin crafting your scenes. To do that, we must move beyond structure and look at some of the nuts and bolts of screenwriting.

SCREENPLAY FORMATTING

Before we get into the nitty gritty of writing a scene, we need to take a moment to talk about **standard screenplay format**. Standard screenplay formatting is the guidelines that Hollywood has developed over the years for what a written screenplay should look like. As guidelines, they can and have been modified to suit various writers' needs, but this formatting has remained basically the same since synch dialogue came to cinema. You should adhere to the current standards if you are a novice writer and want to be taken seriously in the film business. Not using standard format can turn off potential buyers from even reading your script, so it's just common sense not to limit your chances of success from the get go over something so small as formatting. Know the rules, and stick to them.

Using one of the several screenplay formatting software programs out there can free you from having to learn standard formatting, but it's a good idea to understand standard formatting regardless of what software tool you might use. The majority of screenplays written and produced in Hollywood adhere to most, if not all, of the basic formatting guidelines listed below:

- 12-point Courier font
- 1.5 inch left margin (leaving room for punch holes and brads)
- 1-inch right margin (ragged, not justified)
- 1-inch top and bottom margins
- Pages should be numbered in the top right corner, flush to the right margin, a half-inch from the top of the page. The first page is not numbered. The **title page** is not numbered and does not count as page one. The first page to have a number is the second page of the screenplay (third sheet of paper, including the title page), which is numbered as page 2. ⸺

- Dialogue begins 2.5 inches from left side of the page (1 inch from the margin) and breaks at 6 inches from left side of page. You must double space every time dialogue changes from one character to another. Also double space between dialogue and action and dialogue and scene headings, subheaders, and transitions. You do not double space for parentheticals.

- The very first words on the first page are always: FADE IN
- The following screenplay elements are CAPITALIZED:
  - all camera instructions (should be used very sparingly)
  - all sounds, including music (some writers don't do this anymore)
  - all character names the first time they appear in a description/action line
  - every word in the scene header
  - the speaker's name, above each line of dialogue

SCREENPLAY ELEMENTS

Below is a list of the standard screenplay elements (as delineated by screenwriter Mario Moreno and Kay Tuxford of the *Writers' Store*, a Los Angeles institution, now a division of *Writer's Digest*, that every screenwriter should know about), along with some examples. These elements are common to virtually all screenplays, so you need to learn them. If you use a screenwriting software tool like Final Draft (which most screenwriters in Hollywood use), the software will automatically format all these elements for you as you type, but you as a screenwriter should know these definitions and understand when to use these elements.

Scene Heading

Indent: Left: 0.0" (from margin) Width: 6.0"

A scene heading is a one-line description of the location and time of day of a scene, also known as a "slugline". Scene headings should always be in CAPS. The scene heading reveals where (interior/exterior and location) and when (day or night) the following action is taking place.

Example:

```
INT. WRITERS STORE - DAY
```

The above scene heading tells the reader that scene takes place inside the Writers Store in the daytime. You should double space after all scene headings.

Subheader (a type of scene heading)

Indent: Left: 0.0" Width: 6.0"

When a new scene heading is not necessary, but some distinction needs to be made in the action, you can use a subheader. But be sure to use these sparingly, as a script full of subheaders is generally frowned upon.

A good example is when you have a series of quick cuts between two locations, you use the term INTERCUT along with the scene locations instead of writing INT. or EXT. multiple times. Double space after all subheaders.

Action

Indent: Left: 0.0" (from margin) Width: 6.0"

The narrative description of the events of a scene, written in the present tense. Lines of action or narrative description should be single spaced. Double space at the end of all actions.

EXAMPLE:

```
The door opens, and a man, a thirty-something
hipster with attitude to spare, enters.
```

There is no length limit here, but you should try to keep your action lines as tight and brief as possible. Remember, you're writing a screenplay, not a novel, and a screenplay as we've said only needs to be a blueprint for the movie. Only include what is absolutely necessary for a reader to understand what is happening in the scene.

Also, remember that **only things that can be seen and heard by the audience should be included** in the action. You should avoid describing what a character is thinking, as that is something that cannot be easily seen or heard.

Character

Indent: Left: 2.0" (from margin) Width: 4.0"

Character names are CAPITALIZED and always listed above lines of dialogue like this:

```
                    JARED
          Hey, do you have any screenwriting
          software on sale?
```

When a character is first introduced, his name should also be CAPITAL-IZED within the action. For example:

```
The door opens and JARED enters, a thirty-something
hipster with attitude to spare.
```

Minor characters may be designated without proper names, as for example "TAXI DRIVER" or "CUSTOMER".

Dialogue

Indent: Left: 1.0" from margin (2.5" from left side of page) Width: 3.5"

Lines of speech for each character. Dialogue format is used anytime a character is heard speaking, even for off-screen and voice-over dialogue. Dialogue is always single spaced.

Parenthetical

Indent: Left: 1.5" (from margin) Width: 2.5"

A parenthetical is a specific direction for the character speaking, such as an attitude or action. For example:

```
          CHARACTER
        (grimacing)
  Dialogue spoken by character.
```

Parentheticals should be used very rarely, and only if absolutely necessary for two simple reasons. First, if you need to use a parenthetical to convey what's going on with your dialogue, then it probably just needs a good rewrite. Second, it's the director's job to instruct an actor on how to deliver a line, and an actor's job to deliver the line, so don't encroach on their turf unless you feel they won't understand the intent of the dialogue without it.

Extension

Placed after the character's name, in parentheses.

An abbreviated technical note placed after the character's name to indicate how the voice will be heard onscreen. For example, if the character is speaking in a voice-over, it would appear as JARED (V.O.) or JANE (O.S.) for off-screen dialogue.

Transition

Indent: Left: 4.0" (from margin) Width: 2.0"

Transitions are film editing instructions, and generally only appear in a shooting script. Transition verbiage includes:

CUT TO:

DISSOLVE TO:

SMASH CUT:

QUICK CUT:

FADE TO:

As a screenwriter, you should avoid using a transition unless there is no other way to indicate a story element. For example, you might need to use DISSOLVE TO: to indicate that a large amount of time has passed between two scenes.

Shot

Indent: Left: 0.0" (from margin) Width: 6.0"

A shot tells the reader that the focal point within a scene has changed. Like a transition, there's rarely a time when a screenwriter should insert shot directions. That's the director's job.

Examples of Shots:

ANGLE ON—description of what is seen

JANE'S POV—description of what is seen

Beginning with your first notecard, then you can start writing the first scene of your script like this:

```
FADE IN:

INT. WRITERS STORE - DAY

The door opens and JARED, a thirty-something hip-
ster with attitude to spare, enters.

                    JARED
          Hey, do you have any screenwrit-
          ing software on sale? I hear
          Final Draft is pretty good?
```

Learning proper screenplay format is not difficult. Anyone can do it. It's all about capitalizing, spacing, margins, and knowing where to place the header, character names, and dialogue. What is hard is writing a great screenplay, one with a compelling character and plot. To familiarize yourself with what a screenplay should look like, take some time to read screenplays; you can find them on the internet if you look.

CRAFTING SCENES THROUGH CONFLICT

The key to writing a good scene does not lie in proper formatting, unfortunately, though many a novice writer gets hung up on that aspect of the craft. Crafting a great scene, and a great script from those scenes, requires more subtle, creative work. It begins by understanding that **a good scene must do at least these two things:** reveal character and advance the plot. This is the same concept used to define the key elements that make up a story—character and plot. You can't have one without the other, as we've said, and one doesn't supersede the other. You must have both if who want to tell a story, and your goal should be to reveal character and advance the plot in every scene where possible. The key to doing this is to make sure that every scene you write has conflict in it.

Revealing Character

Conflict is critical because it can be used to reveal character by showing the audience who your characters are instead of telling them. That's because conflict should prompt action by a character. It's only when your characters are in real conflict that you can show the audience what the character is made of by showing how they respond to the conflict. Conflict can reveal what the character desires and fears, what they really want or need. Conflict can also reveal basic everyday things like personality or values.

To reveal character, you must know your characters. And one way to do this is to develop a **backstory** for them. Backstory is defined as what has happened to a character before the movie starts. Paul Peditto, screenwriter and author of the blog *scriptgodsmustdie.com* points out three crucial ways that backstory can help you create characters and reveal who they are in the scenes of your script.

- It impacts character dialect and dialogue: The voice of the character; how they talk, the content of their mind.
- It impacts worldview: Education, intelligence or non-intelligence. Prejudices, likes, dislikes, and hates.

- It impacts motivation: Why they do what they do; the reason they behave certain ways in certain situations.

When you first introduce a character, aside from capitalizing their name to adhere to standard screenplay format, you also should add a brief description of the character. This character description is your first chance to reveal something about who that character is to the audience. It's also the first thing the actor playing the role sees.

Not all characters need a full description, especially those that only appear once or twice. Naming them WAITRESS or TAXI DRIVER will tell the reader enough about them. Don't write three lines of description about minor characters. But for your main characters, it's important to craft a useful character description. To do so, focus on the visual essence of the character, get to the core of who they are. Don't settle for vague, generic phrases like *tall, handsome, sexy, cute.* Avoid weak adjectives like *slighty, mildly, somewhat.* Paint a memorable picture and do it in as few words as possible. The first time Ron Woodruff appears in DALLAS BUYERS CLUB, in the opening scene, writers Craig Borten and Melisa Wallack describe the protagonist of their film this way:

```
RON WOODROOF, early 40's, handsome, long sandy
hair, denim clad, worn snakeskin boots, dusty,
cowboy hat, mirrored aviators, is engaged in wild
SEX with a WOMAN.
```

You don't have to go overboard in your character descriptions. Sometimes simple and short is best. The key is to capture the essence of who that character is, not simply what they look like. For example, later in DALLAS BUYERS CLUB, the writers introduce several important characters very simply:

```
Barrow Wilkem rep RICK FERRIS, slick, well-dressed,
gold Rolex, 40s, stands before DR. NATHAN SEVARD,
50's, arrogant, DR. EVE SAKS, early 30s, sophis-
ticated, and five other PHYSICIANS, 40s-60s, all
members of the hospital board.
```

Whatever ways you choose to describe your characters, it's a good idea to spend some quality time creating a backstory for the main characters of your script before you begin writing, so that you know how to write the character's dialogue and actions in your scenes. The goal is to create realistic behavior, behavior that adheres to common sense, physical reality, and psychological truthfulness. This is of course easier said than done, but if you spend a little time creating a backstory for your main characters, you will go a long way toward making them believable to the audience.

Advancing the Plot

Conflict in a scene is best motivated by one of two things: the hero's over-all goal in the story, or a specific goal of a character in the scene. The scene then becomes a struggle or debate between that character and whoever is acting as the antagonistic force in that scene (another character, society, the environment, the character themselves). It's conflict that both reveals character and pushes the plot forward. Make sure that at the very least your scenes are doing one of these two things, and ideally both. Ask yourself what the main plot of the scene is, and then craft the scene around it. And avoid having more than one plot point in the scene. Doing so will keep your story simple and make what's happening easier for the audience to follow.

If when you first write a scene it doesn't seem to have any conflict in it, you must add some. Otherwise it's not a scene, it's just a description of people doing stuff for no good reason. If you can't find the conflict in a scene, that's a sign that the scene should probably be cut from the script, as it serves no dramatic purpose. Remember that conflict is the rocket fuel that writers use to create rising action. This rising action then builds the story arc and character arc through ever more challenging obstacles until the climax of the story is reached.

Polarity

One concept in screenwriting that can help you create conflict in your scene is **emotional polarity**. If you remember your notecards, you'll recall that in the bottom left corner on each one you jotted down who the conflict was between in the scene, and whether the polarity was up or down. A scene with down polarity starts out positively for the hero (happy or upbeat) and ends negatively (sad or downbeat).

The only way to get a scene to go from happy to sad, or sad to happy, is through the conflict between the characters. Most, but not all your scenes, will include the protagonist, but in scenes that don't, conflict is still necessary. Polarity in scenes that don't include the protagonist is determined by how the outcome affects either the protagonist or, occasionally, how it effects the main character of that scene. A scene can also go from bad to worse, or from good to better; all that matters is that it changes from the beginning to the end of the scene.

Genres—What Are They Good For?

Another valuable tool to help you craft the scenes of your film is **genre**. If you are writing a genre movie, you need to understand that there are certain rules, conventions, or tropes that audiences expect to see in specific genres. Blake Snyder listed ten genre types he believed all movies fit. These genres include: *Monster in the House* (horror films like JAWS and ALIEN), *Golden Fleece* (RAIDERS and STAR WARS), *Out of the Bottle* (LIAR LIAR), *Dude with a Problem* (DIE HARD), *Rites of Passage* (coming of age stories like LEGALLY BLONDE), *Buddy Love* (DUMB & DUMBER, RAIN MAN), *Whydunit* (CHINATOWN), *The Fool Triumphant* (FORREST GUMP), *Institutionalized* (ONE FLEW OVER THE CUCKOOS NEST), and *Superhero* (BATMAN).

Each of these genres have certain story requirements based on their history. These required story elements tie into audience expectations. For example, *Monster in the House* movies require that a sin be committed early on that prompts the creation of a supernatural monster. This monster, as Snyder says, will then act like an avenging angel to kill those who committed the sin. So, if you're writing this type of movie, you'll need to develop scenes in your script that fit this genre convention.

If you think you're writing a genre movie, check out Snyder's list in *Save the Cat!* as well as his more in-depth analysis of genre types *Save the Cat! Goes to the Movies*. Genre conventions can be very useful tools for helping writers craft scenes that are well suited for a specific genre type. There's a caveat however to relying too heavily on genre conventions. Adhering too closely to a genre's tropes can result in clichéd storytelling. A script full of clichés will most likely bore a reader, because it will be too predictable. There won't be any surprises, and audiences love surprises. Remember the adage *new wine in old bottles*, and try to satisfy or subvert genre conventions by putting your own unique twist on them.

Every Scene a Little Movie

Almost every scene in a film can be thought of as a little movie. Scenes, like stories, have a beginning, middle, and end. As we'll see later in this chapter, many scenes either omit or radically trim the beginning and end, but it's helpful to remember, especially when writing your **first draft**, that your scenes should have a structure to them. Every scene can be viewed as a little movie, as we've said, and so in every scene of your script the main character of that scene (usually the protagonist) should have a goal. The emotion of the scene will be determined by whether that goal is achieved or not. If the lead character achieves their goal in the scene, the scene is viewed as an upbeat one, with a positive polarity. If the goal isn't achieved, it will be felt as a downbeat scene, with negative polarity.

A great example of this notion of treating every scene as a little movie occurs in GET OUT in the scene where TSA agent Rod goes to the police to tell them that Chris is missing. The scene could exist as a short movie all on its own, it's so well structured. It has a setup (Rod and the woman detective meet), rising action (Rod struggles to tell his story, and to get her to believe it), climax complete with a twist (the detective calls in her fellow cops, so they can hear the Rod's story, as if she believes him finally), and a resolution (they all burst out laughing at Rod, like he's crazy). Notice too that it's a scene that does not include the main character, yet it works to move the story forward, humorously upping the tension. It also helps create a character arc for Rod in the overall story. He moves from goofy buddy, to conspiracy theorist, to a friend doing the practical, smart thing (going to the cops) for his friend. Rod's arc is so complete it even includes a low point—the cops don't believe him and his friend is now more likely than ever to die.

The opening scene in RAIDERS is another classic example of a scene feeling like a mini-movie. The scene has a setup (Indy entering the cave with his allies), rising action (the ever-increasing obstacles that stand between Indy and his goal, retrieving the golden idol), conflict (between Indy and the environment, Indy and Satipo, and Indy and Belloq), and climax (Indy escaping the giant killer rolling stone). It even has a resolution or denouement, when Belloq takes away the idol and tells Indy he will never outsmart Belloq. Most scenes you write don't need to be this all-encompassing, but it's not a bad idea to create scenes like this, using the concept of every scene a little movie, when you are writing your own scenes. The more a scene can do for you, the more efficient it is dramatically, and the better your overall screenplay will be.

Some writing gurus, like the brilliant Robert McKee (author of STORY), will tell you that if one scene starts positive and ends negative, the next should start negative and end positive (and vice versa). This will connect the scenes in your script together like the teeth of a saw pointed diagonally upwards, and will help you create the necessary rising action you need to reach the climax of your story. This is a good goal to aim for, but it isn't strictly necessary and certainly not always adhered to. It is wise however to note that how the scene before the one you're writing ends will have an impact on how the audience enters the next scene, emotionally. Knowing this should help you decide how the next scene begins. This concept is sometimes called **scenic proximity**, and it's a good one to keep in mind as you start to string scenes together.

Story Beats and Emotional Beats

Another important concept to remember when writing your scenes is that scenes, like movies, have beats. In a scene, there can be two types of beats: **story beats** and **emotional beats**. Again, this goes back to the fundamental elements of storytelling; plot and character. A scene will normally only have one story beat, or plot point. This story beat is usually reflected in the climax of the scene, and is the result of the conflict in that scene (remember our adage, every scene a little movie).

Scenes can have multiple emotional beats (also known as **character beats**) depending on the length, but these beats should build like the rising action in your story to one emotional high point in the scene. These rising emotional beats are driven by the conflict as well, and will often lead to a climactic moment or turning point in the scene. If your scene doesn't have at least one of these beats, story or emotional, it's not really a scene. You must either create these beats in the scene, or else cut the scene as it serves no purpose in your script.

The *"I'll have what she's having"* scene in WHEN HARRY MET SALLY is a good one to look at as an example of a scene with both a story beat and emotional beats. The story beat is a very clear one, the stating of the theme: men and women can't be friends because sex always gets in the way. Stating this theme sets up the dramatic premise of the entire story: can Harry and Sally be just friends? This question sets up the conflict between Harry and Sally from this point forward. The scene itself has a nice polarity too. It starts on a down note, when Sally asks Harry, "What do you do with these women (you sleep with)? Just get out of bed and leave?" The status quo is laid out in some simple exposition in his reply: "Just have an early meeting, a dentist appointment, a squash game." "You don't play squash," she says. "They don't know that, they just met me," Harry replies, and then we get the first emotional beat of the scene, when she reacts in disgust. This emotional beat is the end of the first act of this scene, and turns the scene in a new direction, a debate over fake orgasms and cocky men.

This back and forth, this conflict between what Sally believes and what Harry believes builds until Sally ultimately wins the argument by faking an orgasm in the crowded diner, shaming Harry into silence. The scene ends on an upbeat note, though not for Harry ironically, when a woman who's watched this scene unfold from another table tells the waitress, "I'll have what she's having".

Get in Late, Get Out Early

Another useful tool or trick of the trade for writing good scenes is to trim or cut the heads and tails, the beginnings and endings, of scenes. For scenes that occur in the middle of acts, the audience doesn't always need to see the entire beginning or end of the scene as it might play out normally. They can infer what the beginning was, or guess at the ending. Audiences today are smart enough to connect the dots between scenes for themselves.

There's a commonly used phrase used by writers for this kind of truncation of a scene: starting *in media res*. The phrase is Latin for "in the midst of things". In storytelling, it's the practice of beginning a story, or a scene, without any setup or exposition, but instead in the middle of a crucial situation. The scene or story continues directly forward, and the exposition of earlier events is either completely removed from the narrative or is supplied later on with flashbacks.

Beginning a story *in medias res* began in literature with Homer, another one of those clever ancient Greeks. In his epic narrative *The Iliad*, Homer begins his story of the Trojan War dramatically with a quarrel between Achilles and Agamemnon. The Latin poet and critic Horace pointed out how doing so allowed Homer to create immediate interest in his audience, in contrast to starting the story with the birth of Achilles, the story's earliest chronological event.

This same principle can be applied to almost any scene you write. The opening of RAIDERS is again a perfect example. We don't need to see Indiana Jones in his office at school, preparing for his journey to South America. We don't need to see him fly down there, get off the plane, find his guides, hike hours through the jungle, and finally arrive outside the cave where the scene begins. Instead screenwriter Lawrence Kasdan just plunges us in to the middle of this action, and we as audience members must grab ahold of the story and hang on for dear life until the opening beat is concluded. And by then we have been swept up in the narrative, and are ready and willing to go along for the rest of the ride to see what happens. Kasdan does this many times throughout RAIDERS, most notably again in the scene where we are first introduced to Marion Ravenwood, in the middle of a drinking contest.

Trimming heads and tails of scenes removes unnecessary moments, moments that lack drama or importance to a scene or to the story. It is, as we will explain in more detail later, one of the best tools a writer has at his disposable when he begins the challenging work of rewriting and polishing his or her first draft of a screenplay. Trimming heads and tails also helps with the pacing of the screenplay. The faster you want the pace to move from scene to scene, the more you may want to trim the beginning and end of the scenes in the sequence or act you're writing.

Leave Them Hanging

This tool is a subset of the *get in late get out early* concept. When you trim endings, it's important to know where to make the edit. The choice of how far back from the end of the scene as written you should cut is both an artistic, creative choice, but also a practical, narrative one. You'll notice that if you trim the ending back far enough to cut the resolution of the scene that this will leave the reader or audience asking themselves, what happened? You might worry that you can't leave people hanging like that, but this isn't necessarily a bad thing at all when crafting scenes.

In fact, cutting the resolution of a scene can work to your advantage as you begin stringing scenes together. The reason is fairly obvious. By trimming off the resolution of the scene, you force the audience to become more involved in the story by making them ask themselves the same question you have, *what is going to happen next*? If you do this well, your audience will get so involved in the story, they'll forget they're reading a script or watching a movie. In the task of plot construction and the crafting of scenes, sometimes questions are better than answers. Be careful however not to remove the main story point, or the key emotional beat of the scene when trimming, otherwise your scene will have no purpose (and a scene with no character or plot function should be cut).

Planting and Paying Off

Another very powerful tool for crafting scenes is the concept of **planting and paying off**. This concept, more commonly known in literature as **foreshadowing**, is very useful when constructing sequences, acts, and entire stories from individual scenes. This is because planting and paying off helps tie an earlier scene to a later one thus giving the script a kind of narrative logic or flow. This can be done by placing something, an object, a line of dialogue, an idea, a character trait or action in an earlier scene, something that doesn't appear on its surface to be important. Then in a subsequent scene, you bring the audience back to that seed you planted earlier in a way that makes them remember what they saw earlier, and better yet realize its sudden, newfound importance—in other words by paying it off.

Good screenwriters always use this tool when constructing their screenplays, because it keeps the audience engaged in the story. It's also important to note here that sometimes these moments come to you after you've written the entire first draft, in the rewrite stage. Adding plants and payoffs in the rewrite stage can often be easier for that reason, so keep that in mind as you work on your own scripts. Some examples of planting and paying off follow:

Get Out

Chris and Rose hit a deer early on in the film. This plants the deer and the accident in the audiences' minds, and it foreshadows what we later learn happened to Chris's mom—she was killed by a hit and run driver. We see the stuffed head of a deer again, later when Chris is held captive in the sunken place, reminding us again of this awful event, and making us even more worried for Chris.

Rose's brothers dialogue at the dinner table about MMA fighting is another instance of planting, as is Rose's line about her brother wanting to put Chris in a headlock. Both pay off in the final, brutal fight scene between Chris and Rose's brother.

The Secret Life of Walter Mitty

Walter's mom's clementine cake is planted early on in a scene that introduces Walter's sister, and screenwriter Steve Conrad comes back to it again when Walter lands on the fishing trawler and is offered clementine cake by a crew member. This in turn pays off when Walter finds out his mom and Sean know each other. The two are connected by her clementine cake, a favorite of both Walter's and Sean's.

A Christmas Story

Repeating the line "You'll shoot your eye out kid" in multiple scenes plants the notion in the audiences' minds that Ralphie better be careful what he's wishing for, and it's paid off, very nicely, when Ralphie tries out his new Red Rider BB gun near the end, and nearly shoots his eye out.

The Twist

There's one more type of scene we should discuss before moving on, and that's the **reversal** scene, more commonly known as the **twist**. A twist, or reversal, is something that occurs in the story that surprises the audience, usually because they were expecting something else to happen. You can set up these expectations using the concept of planting and paying off. The difference is that instead of the audience getting what they expected, you give them the exact opposite, something unexpected. Most people like surprises in real life, but movie audiences especially love them.

According to Robert McKee, every scene can be improved by utilizing this basic notion of reversal or surprise. In his book *Story*, McKee calls this "opening the gap". For McKee, this notion works on the smallest of levels to help build conflict in individual scenes. Character A tells character B something, or acts in opposition to character B in some way, and then Character B responds. For the scene to build, Character B's response should act as a kind of surprise to Character A, and this unexpected response acts to ratchet up the conflict in the scene until the emotional high point of the scene is reached.

Think of the opening scene of RAIDERS again. When Indy asks Sapito to throw him the whip, Sapito surprises him by saying, "Throw me the idol." When Indy does throw him the idol, Sapito again surprises Indy by dropping the whip and running out of the cave. Each response opens the gap in the conflict, until it's finally resolved a moment later, by the final surprise—Sapito's gruesome death.

The twist can act on this micro level, or it can act on the macro story level. If the writer has been doing his job, and built tension through conflict, ever-increasing obstacles, and rising action, the audience will begin to expect a certain outcome to the story. We see this most often done well in the suspense or thriller genre, but also in horror and comedy too. In LEGALLY BLONDE, we get multiple story reversals. One of the funniest occurs when Elle teaches Paulette how to do the "bend and snap" to catch a man's interest. A whole scene is built around it as a setup or plant. Then when it comes time for Paulette to put the ploy into practice, the writers deliver a wonderful reversal as Paulette breaks the UPS man's nose when she snaps her head up into his face.

Scene Types

As you begin to write your scenes, you'll also soon discover that there are various types of scenes. In laying out our 16 beats, we already defined several: the opening scene, the catalyst scene, the clarifying the problem scene, and the metaphorically dead scene. There's also the final scene, or the takeaway. Each one of these scene types serves a specific function, so it's important as you are moving through your notecards to think about whether the scene you're writing fits one of these types. Each scene you write also fits into a sequence, and an act, and you should always keep that in mind as well when you're writing a scene.

Exposition Scenes

For example, a scene that occurs during the first sequence of your movie, in act one, will either be an opening scene, or a scene that helps establish the status quo. An example of the latter is often called an **exposition** scene, as its main purpose is to give the audience or reader an understanding of your main character's status quo—that is, who they are, and what they're like (flaws included), at the beginning of the movie. Exposition scenes, sometimes referred to as **laying pipe** in Hollywood screenwriting parlance, give the audience valuable information that helps them connect the dots in a story. Exposition scenes focus more on plot than character.

The scenes that depict Elle Wood's sorority life in LEGALLY BLONDE are basically expository scenes. They set up who she is (president of the sorority), what she wants (a marriage proposal), and where we're at (a university in Los Angeles). The scene in RAIDERS where Brody and Indy meet the Army Intelligence officers in Act One is another classic example of an exposition scene. That scene exists to tell us what the Ark of the Covenant is, why it's important, and who's after it. It has other functions too, like confirming that Dr. Jones is an expert on archeology and the Ark, as well as planting information about Abner Ravenwood, Indy's former mentor, but its main purpose is to lay pipe, as they say in Hollywood.

Opening Scenes

Opening scenes, as we mentioned in Chapter Six, have more to do with setting the audience expectations for the rest of the film than they do for the laying out of your plot. Thus tone, theme, and/or character should be emphasized. Opening scenes may not have a story beat in them, but if they don't they should have emotional beats. It's also worth noting that most studio executives have short attention spans, so the first five pages can make or break a script as that may be all they read of it.

Opening scenes come in several types as well. Tim Long of *ScreenplayStory. com* lists a few, including the **teaser** (JAWS is the classic opening teaser scene example, also MEMENTO and FIGHT CLUB), theme focused openings (LORD

OF WAR, A FEW GOOD MEN, DALLAS BUYERS CLUB), tone focused openings (GOODFELLAS, THERE'S SOMETHING ABOUT MARY), and openings that reveal crucial **backstory** (GET OUT, UNFORGIVEN, UP). Some opening scenes will focus on character (THE WIZARD OF OZ, THE SECRET LIFE OF WALTER MITTY, SEVEN). There's also openings that do all of these (RAIDERS OF THE LOST ARK is the perfect example).

Character Driven Scenes

Some scenes in a movie have very little to do with the plot, but are more focused on revealing who a character is. These are often called character scenes. Character scenes don't always have a story beat, but they will almost always have emotional beats. The opening scene in THE SECRET LIFE OF WALTER MITTY is a good example. The scene does little in the way of advancing the plot, but it tells us a great deal about who Walter is—nerdy, solitary, lonely, and a wildly imaginative dreamer. Character scenes are often used in the first act to tell the audience who the main character is and what they're like—their flaws, quirks, unique personality traits.

Character scenes can also serve to connect the audience to the character by making them sympathize with that character. Remember that the basic premise of most films is a story about someone we care about (someone who's likeable or watchable). One specific type of character scene that does this well is what is now known, thanks to Blake Snyder, as a "save the cat" scene. A "save the cat" scene is one where we see the hero do something nice that makes us like him, like saving a cat that's stuck up in a tree or helping an old lady cross the street. It may have nothing to do with the plot at all, but when audiences see a scene like this, especially early on, they end up saying to themselves, "I want to follow this person's story."

This type of scene works even with an otherwise unlikeable character. A great example of this comes early in DALLAS BUYERS CLUB when Ron is at work, and is told to check out an accident on an oil rig where he works. When he gets there, he sees a man with his leg caught in a machine. The man is an illegal alien, has no insurance, and Ron has just shown us earlier in the scene that he's a racist, but instead of letting the man suffer, and possibly even die, Ron forces the foreman to call for an ambulance. Right then the audience knows that even if Ron is a bigot, somewhere inside him lies a decent heart.

Another classic example of a character driven scene occurs in THE WIZARD OF OZ when Dorothy sings "Somewhere Over the Rainbow". This scene's major function is to establish Dorothy's emotional state at the beginning of the film. It tells us something about who she is by revealing her deepest desire, and helps connect the audience to her emotionally.

Action Scenes

Certain genre movies have specific types of scenes that appear in virtually all movies of that genre. Action movies like DIE HARD or ALIENS are full of action scene **set pieces**. Action scenes usually have story beats in them, but don't always have character beats. These scenes are designed to help satisfy the audience's expectations for a certain type or genre of film, as well as to provide the kind of entertaining spectacle that only cinema can provide. BLACK PANTHER, a superhero genre film, has several terrific action scenes in the beginning of Act Two that are terrific examples of action set pieces. The first occurs in a Hong Kong casino (Hong Kong martial arts movies are chock full of action scenes that exist mostly for the sheer thrill of the scene). The second occurs immediately after when the Black Panther and his sister are involved in a car chase with one of the villains. Both scenes advance the plot, but their primary function is to thrill the audience. Audiences expect scenes like these in superhero, action movies. These types of action-focused scenes often occur in the beat Blake Snyder calls *Fun and Games*, or what we've defined as beat 7, the *Try Again, But Harder This Time* beat. They also often occur in the *Final Confrontation* story beat, in Sequence 8 of Act Three.

Dialogue Scenes

Another type of scene is the dialogue driven scene. These scenes can be especially tricky to do well, as they often involve characters who aren't doing anything but talking, and so lack movement, which can be a big problem, as we discussed in Chapter Two. When done well, as in the "*I'll have what she's having*" scene in WHEN HARRY MET SALLY, dialogue scenes can both advance the plot by giving out important exposition or backstory to the audience, and reveal character through conflict, attitude, tone and word choices. Dialogue scenes ideally should have both a story beat and emotional beats to make up for the fact that there's little action in such scenes. The dialogue scene from WHEN HARRY MET SALLY mentioned also articulates the theme of the movie, that men and women can't be just friends because sex gets in the way.

Quentin Tarantino is a master of the dialogue driven scene. The "*Royale with cheese*" scene between the two hitmen played by John Travolta and Samuel L.

Jackson is a perfect example of how to use a dialogue scene in a script. The two men are driving in a car on their way to deliver a terrifying message from drug dealer Marcellus, so can't move much. As they drive, Travolta starts discussing the French version of the Big Mac. It's a funny, entertaining scene, full of great dialogue. It reveals something about who both characters are, and it moves the story along as well.

Another classic example of a great dialogue scene occurs in JAWS (screenplay by Peter Benchley and Carl Gottlieb, based on the novel by Peter Benchley), when Quint regales Hooper and Brody with his World War II story about the sinking of the USS Indianapolis. The scene is riveting as much for Robert Shaw's brilliant acting as it is for the harrowingly terrifying story of a ship full of men eaten by ravenous sharks. Novice writers should be careful when writing scenes like this, however. When the dialogue isn't incredibly sharp and vivid, and if it doesn't reveal something crucial or important about the character, a long **monologue** like Quint's final speech in this scene (which runs about 2 minutes) will bring a movie to a screeching halt by killing the pace. Action defines character in film as much, if not more, than dialogue, so dialogue that slows down or stops the action for long intervals should be used judiciously.

As you may have figured out, great scenes serve more than one function in a screenplay. The opening of RAIDERS not only establishes the tone of the film (action adventure, comedy), but it also sets up the nature of the lead character: the heroic, death defying Indiana Jones, who is afraid to trust others because he's gotten burned— *"Throw me the whip, and I throw you the idol"*—and it sets up one of the main conflicts (Jones vs. Belloq), as well as revealing Jones biggest fear (snakes). Your goal should be to craft scenes that reveal character and advance the plot in as creative a way as you can find, and string these scenes together until you have a complete draft of your screenplay.

WRITING THE FIRST DRAFT

A screenplay is the blueprint for a movie. Notice I did not use the word "just" in that sentence. To say a screenplay is "just" a blueprint for a movie would be an insult to the incredible amount of work it takes to write a good screenplay, as well as to the beauty that can be found in any good blueprint. But no matter how good your blueprint is, it's still not a house. A house is a three-dimensional rendering of that two-dimensional document. The same thing goes for screenplays.

If you've taken the time to work your way through Part One of this book, you now have the basic understanding of how to create a well-structured screenplay. If you followed through on all the exercises, you've now done it once. The story you have created is simple (as proven by the logline). The acts break where they should and how they should (as proven by your three act breakdown and your eight sequence layout). The beats are all there in the right order (per your 16 major beats), and you have just enough scenes, not too many or too few, to create an entire screenplay (as evidenced by the 40 or so scenes you created on notecards). The next step is to put your fingers on the keyboard and write the first draft of your script.

When you start writing your first draft, you should keep a couple things in mind. First, write quickly. Craft your scenes as you notecarded them, and use the tools discussed in this chapter to help you do so. As you write the first draft of your script, try not to be a critic. Your goal in this step should be to get the first draft finished. That alone is no small achievement, and it takes time and effort to do it. If you constantly second-guess yourself, stop and start, stop and re-start, the process will get frustrating, and the effort will become counterproductive. You will have plenty of time to critique your first draft after you've finished it. Work fast, and write every day, or as often as you can, so that you can feel the rush of excitement and use that adrenaline as energy to fuel your effort. Set a goal for how long you want to take to finish the draft. Three weeks is not impossible, and three months not unreasonable. Don't let the writing of the first draft drag on too long however, or you might lose momentum and never finish. Once you do finish, sit back, smile, and relax. Put the script away for at least a week, if not a month (easier said than done), and then start thinking about the next phase in the process—the rewrite.

EXERCISES

Exercise 1: Look over your notecards, and make a note on each about what type of scene it might be: Opening, exposition, action, dialogue, character, or reversal.

Exercise 2: Write a page or two of backstory for the main characters of your script.

Exercise 3: Find one scene that fits each of these scene types—exposition, action, dialogue, character—and write that scene in standard screenplay format.

Exercise 4: Looking at the notecards for your script, make some notes about where you can use a reversal or twist in a scene.

Exercise 5: Look for a couple scenes where you can effectively use the plant and payoff concept, and note specifically what you need to plant where, and how to pay it off.

Exercise 6: Take your first notecard and write that opening scene. Focus on what type of opening you want, and see if you can make the opening scene accomplish more than one thing. Make sure you adhere to standard screenplay format.

Exercise 7: Write the first draft of your script, based on your notecards, and the notes you made in answering the questions above. Note that this exercise alone could take you several weeks, even months to complete. Don't expect to knock out an entire screenplay, even a first draft in a day or two.

FURTHER READINGS:

Make a Scene by Jordan Rosenfeld
Story by Robert McKee

The
Rewrite(s)

Why do you need to rewrite your script, especially after you spent so much time writing the first draft? Why should you bother, especially if you worked hard on creating a well-structured story from logline to notecards? The answer is because it's a near certainty that the first draft you just completed almost certainly sucks. Many a young screenwriter finds this thought a major downer. They think that because they've done all the hard work of creating the structure and then writing the script, their job is finished. Just type up the script based on the notecards and you're done. Unfortunately, that's almost never enough to make your screenplay a good one. Here's a great quote from novelist Max Gladstone about this very issue:

> [F]or every draft you think is great when you put it to bed that first time, you'll write one that just doesn't work. Where you know, when the last line comes, that you've committed a crime against God and literature and the only thing for it is to slink into a tiny shadowy cubby hole to stew in your own sweat and hope nobody notices.

> The funny thing about those drafts is, I mean, yes, sometimes they need more work than the ones that flow like honey. Sometimes. But they both need work, and when you start off thinking, no matter what this is, no matter how I feel about it now, I'll need to work to make it better? Then the despair isn't nearly so sharp. If the [story] is broken, and you know it, that's just one more reason to throw yourself at edits. In a way it even helps. Because you have less attachment to the first draft, you pay more attention to structure, timing, language—to the architecture of acts and the necessities of character and plot.

Why then do most first drafts suck? This is an age-old question asked by virtually every screenwriter who ever put fingers to keyboard. If screenplays are structure, and they are, then why isn't a solid structure enough to make a good movie? And why if you put in the effort to create a solid structure is your first draft going to inevitably be bad? The answer is that the key to writing a good script (after you've nailed the logline, acts, sequences, beats, and scene notecards) is the **rewrite**. The thought of rewriting a script scares most novices to death, so they either simply ignore that part of the process, or else give up before they're truly finished. And that is unfortunate, because all good writers know, ***writing is rewriting***. They are one and the same, part of the process that takes you from idea to finished product. If you skip this final phase of the process, the rewrite stage, you should expect to fail.

So how exactly do you go about rewriting your first draft? What are you actually rewriting? What needs changing? What are you adding, or more likely cutting? How do you make these editorial decisions? Doug Richardson, screenwriter of DIE HARD 2: DIE HARDER, the sequel to DIE HARD, has this to say about the reasons for rewriting your script:

> My primary mantra is always *don't be boring and make sure the reader wants to turn the page.* How is that done? By rewriting. And by that I mean being brutally honest about my own ability to fall in love with my own words.

You rewrite to sharpen the structure of your story; improve the pace; eliminate boring, unnecessary description; improve turgid, cliché dialogue; look for ways to satisfy or subvert a genre's conventions. You search for ways to surprise the audience. In short, you rewrite to make your screenplay better. The following are some ways to do that, focusing on the two main aspects of all stories, plot and character.

GETTING FEEDBACK

Many young writers are afraid to show their work to others, for fear of receiving criticism. If you are one of these writers, you need to get past your fear of being critiqued. It's a part of the business of screenwriting, and used properly feedback can be invaluable. Writer, director, and script consultant Timothy Cooper, writing in *Script Magazine*, offers a list of common first draft issues you need to be aware of and fix in your rewrite. Here are a few of them:

1. Characters are described in excruciating detail.
2. The scene begins at the very beginning of the exchange, rather than the middle.
3. Typos.
4. People say exactly what they mean.
5. The actual action of the scene is unclear.
6. Formatting issues.
7. Much of the information is impossible to actually show on the screen.
8. Long chunks of text.
9. An unimportant character is given too much weight.
10. No major conflict.
11. Unnecessary parentheticals.
12. Clichéd dialogue.

Cooper also offers some guidelines to follow as you begin the rewrite phase. After rewarding yourself for finishing the first draft (and it's no small accomplishment, so celebrate it!), and putting out of your mind any thoughts of trying to sell your script now Cooper suggests the following steps: get feedback, hold a staged reading, then start the rewrite.

Getting feedback doesn't mean looking for praise from your best friend, nor does it mean giving it to that one person you know hates everything. It's best to get feedback from people who are already familiar with either writing or reading screenplays; those who aren't familiar with screenwriting or filmmaking aren't going to be able to give you very much useful feedback. If there's no one like that in your circle of friends, you can find plenty of resources online (more on that in Part Three of this book). You might even think about paying for professional feedback from an experienced script consultant, if you're serious about being a screenwriter.

If you have a few friends who have acted before, whether in films or on stage, getting them together to read your script aloud can be an extremely helpful thing to do before you begin your rewrite. Staged readings, often called a **table read** in Hollywood, are used by almost every television show to sharpen scripts. A great many feature film scripts also do read-throughs with the director and actors before they shoot. Hearing someone read your words out loud, especially if they have some acting experience, will give you a great deal of useful information. You'll hear what descriptions or scenes go on too long, what dialogue doesn't work, and what action is confusing. You should quietly listen and take notes as you follow along in the script. When you've finished the read through, ask for feedback, too. Compare this feedback with the feedback you got from script readers. You'll get a strong sense of what people did and didn't like and insight into what you need to change or improve.

When you finally begin to rewrite your first draft, remember this: professional screenwriters go through dozens of drafts for each script, and can take months or even years to finish a screenplay. You may not have that kind of time or level of commitment, but in the real world, that is exactly what it will take to be successful.

ADDRESSING PLOT PROBLEMS

The first thing you will notice, even as soon as the first draft, is if the story is working. Is your structure sound? Do your scenes have a logical flow? Does the plot work? Remember back to the fairytale method of story structure. Do the scenes, sequences and acts of the story connect. *Once upon a time this was going on... Until one day something surprising happened... And because of this the hero went on a journey... Until finally they succeeded... And ever since they've lived happily ever after...* That kind of logical flow is crucial to creating a working plot. If your scenes merely feel episodic, as in *this happened, then this happened, then this happened,* you have a plot problem and it needs to be addressed. Other common plot problems are discussed below with respect to the acts where they most often appear.

Common Act One Problems

The Opening Doesn't Hook the Reader

Does your opening scene or sequence hook the audience? In today's Hollywood, grabbing the audience by the lapels as soon as they sit down is standard operating procedure, and has been so since JAWS. If you're making an independent film, you can get away with a more leisurely, relaxed opening, but you should still be thinking about how you are connecting your protagonist with the audience.

Opening scenes are some of the most rewritten scenes of an entire script. If you're getting notes that readers don't care about your hero, this is a good place to start fixing that problem. If you want a studio to buy your script, or an agent or producer to get excited about it, you have to hook them quickly. There are many examples throughout this book of great openings (RAIDERS, GET OUT, JAWS, CASABLANCA). Watch them again, and see how long it takes you to get hooked, and more importantly what the writer has done to hook you.

A Weak or Late-Arriving Catalyst

Another common Act One problem is a weak catalyst. If you spent time outlining the script, you probably have a catalyst in your first draft, but is the catalyst a big enough jolt? The catalyst should completely upset the hero's status quo to be effective. It should demand the protagonist's attention, immediately. If it doesn't, you need to turn the catalyst's impact up a notch or several.

Another common catalyst problem is that it's happening too late. The scenes of the first sequence (the opening and set up where you establish the status quo) may be running too long, or you may have too many of them. This will cause your audience to start wondering what the story is about. They are subconsciously looking for the main story thread that they should be following, and if you aren't giving it to them, they will either get lost or worse yet, become bored. As you begin your rewrite, work on getting to the catalyst by page 15 at the latest, and ideally by page 12. Doing so gets the story rolling, because the catalyst is where the main story problem is first introduced.

No Doubt or Debate Before the Decision to Act

The last, and least obvious of the Act One problems we'll look at involves the second sequence and especially the *doubt, debate, and decision* beat. Novice writers will often skip over this beat entirely in a rush to get to the second act. This sequence is not just a bunch of talk about what the hero should do and how to do it. It's not a single scene of the hero expressing doubts about taking action (JAWS), or of allies cautioning the hero to look before they leap (RAIDERS). This sequence is about the hero working through their doubts and exploring their options, and as we said in Chapter Six, it can take two forms depending on whether the hero is a reluctant one (like Ron Woodruff in DALLAS BUYERS CLUB) or an over eager one (like Elle in LEGALLY BLONDE).

Ask yourself if the debate sequence is doing what it's supposed to be doing in your script? Does the reluctant hero look for the easy way out, or try to ignore or minimize the problem suddenly at hand? Does the gung-ho eager beaver do the logical things they need to in order to move into the second act world (as Elle does in LEGALLY BLONDE)? This second sequence of the script is often comprised of more than one scene in which the protagonist actively tries to deal with the enormously unexpected challenge brought about by the catalyst.

Protagonists shouldn't just leap into the scary unknown world of Act Two immediately, without some conflict with allies voicing serious reservations. They should do the things that you or I might do in a hasty, obvious way to try to deal with the issue. This action helps make them relatable (likeable) to the audience. Also make sure your protagonist is making a willful choice to enter the Act Two, antithesis world. This sequence is the entire second half of Act One, so you can use a couple scenes to have the hero take the necessary steps to try to figure out, solve, or reverse the catalyst. Doing so (as in LEGALLY BLONDE and DALLAS BUYERS CLUB) helps go a long way to cementing your audience's caring about what happens to the hero.

Common Act Two Problems

Act Two can be the most daunting to write, simply because it's the longest of the three acts. Don't let that fact overwhelm you. Remember Act Two is built from four sequences and eight story beats, and so as you're reviewing your second act make sure you are hitting all those beats, and that the sequences are fleshed out.

Lack of Conflict

This is often the biggest issue with first drafts from novice writers. To deal with it in the rewrite stage, ask yourself if you have created sufficient conflict in Act Two? If not, you'll need to address that. Remember conflict doesn't just mean characters shouting (or shooting) at each other—it can be more subtle as in LEGALLY BLONDE, THE SECRET LIFE OF WALTER MITTY, or GET OUT. But conflict must be there in every scene. As you rewrite your first draft, work on enhancing the conflict in every scene. Can you add obstacles, complications, twists, or reversals to the scenes in Act Two to improve the conflict in those scenes, and thus heighten the overall conflict in your script?

An Underdeveloped Antagonist

Another important element that can improve the conflict in your story is the antagonist. A strong antagonistic force will help you put "hurdles, roadblocks, mine fields, potholes, and everything else you can think of in your hero's path", as George R. Wolfe writes in *Script Magazine*, forcing them to struggle to move the story forward to the climax and resolution. To achieve this, a writer needs to create powerful antagonistic forces (not always a specific character), which are acting against the protagonist, in what scriptwriter Erik Bork (BAND OF BROTHERS) calls in his blog on screenwriting, *Flying Wrestler*, a "punch-coun-terpunch" kind of struggle. As the hero and villain engage in conflict, the story moves back and forth, each character reacting to the other, adjusting and trying new things, so that the situation continuously evolves. Make sure in your rewrite that you have the protagonist and antagonist constantly adjusting to what the other does, otherwise your script may suffer from another problem that often occurs in a first draft—not enough rising action.

Author and script guru Chuck Wendig has a list of things you should look closely at when writing a villain on his *Terrible Minds* blog, referenced at the end of this chapter:

- Create antagonists who are real people with real problems, powerful wants, and genuine motivations.
- Antagonists should not be just plot devices you use as obstacles for the hero to overcome.
- The villain can't be ridiculously all powerful; they can't be too weak either. They must be a real challenge to the hero.
- Your villain's personality should contrast the hero's in every way; they are the antithesis to the protagonist's thesis.
- Spend time with the antagonist, develop their character in scenes built around them.
- Connect the audience to the villain emotionally; give the audience genuine reasons to like and hate them.
- Just as the hero can have a "save the cat" moment, give the villain a "kick the cat" moment.
- Avoid having villains give long, boring, expository speeches that explain the plot or their motivations.

The bottom line with all these suggestions is to examine the way you've written your villain in the first draft, and see where and how you can make them more believable and effective.

Not Enough Rising Action

As we said in Part One, the stakes for the protagonist must be high, as should the degree of difficulty in achieving their goal. The process of trying to achieve the goal needs to build to a breaking point in the climax. A lot of scripts, however, suffer from having an overall story that doesn't really build enough tension, with a level of conflict that stays too much the same throughout. In short, the action doesn't rise enough.

One way to fix this, as Eric Bork suggests, is to make sure the game changes for the main character in virtually every scene. By this Bork means that the status of the overall problem and goal—and where the hero is at in trying to achieve it— must continuously be growing more difficult and challenging. The conflict cannot just stay at one level. The tension, through rising action, must build otherwise you have what feels like a stalemate. Make sure as you rewrite your script that it has sufficient rising action if you want the audience to remain engrossed in the story throughout the second act.

Study GET OUT for how to raise the tension in a story slowly, and gradually until the midpoint, and then crank it up to 11 by the time the climax arrives. In the beginning there's barely any conflict at all (outside of the opening scene), just enough to get us interested in the characters. Once Chris arrives at Rose's parents, writer/director Jordan Peele begins to up the tension, slowly at first, until there's a major crescendo at the midpoint, when Andre yells at Chris to *"Get out!"* From the midpoint on, the story turns decidedly darker and more violent until it reaches a final, ultimate crescendo as Chris tries to escape the house, and ends up nearly killing Rose to do so. GET OUT is a masterpiece in creating rising action.

A Weak Midpoint

One of the best ways to tackle an Act Two rewrite is to realize that right smack in the middle of the act is an important turning point—the midpoint. With this midpoint in mind, you can think of Act Two as having two parts, the one before the midpoint, and the one after. That midpoint acts as a fulcrum that pivots your story and helps you build tension through rising action.

As you look at your first draft, ask yourself if you have created a strong midpoint for your script, and is it effective? As the hero attempts to achieve their goal, they find the going getting tougher. Part of the reason is because the hero doesn't yet understand the full nature of the problem, they only think they do. It's not until the midpoint that the problem will be clarified for the hero. The specific story beat to evaluate in your rewrite is the *clarifying the problem* story beat. Have you clarified the problem for your hero at the midpoint?

GET OUT is a great example of a midpoint clarifying the problem for the hero. This beat occurs in the backyard party scene, where Chris meets another

African-American, Andre, who at first appears to have successfully "assimilated" to this white crowd. When Chris accidentally flashes Andre with his cell phone camera, Andre appears to lose his mind for a moment and charges Chris, yelling, "*Get out!*". At this moment, Chris's problem has been clarified. He needs to get the heck out of there before he is turned into another Andre, Walter or Georgina.

Knowing how you want the movie to end can also help you improve your midpoint. Remember this story beat often mirrors the climax, in that what will eventually occur in the climax is the opposite of what has just occurred at the midpoint. Also remember there are two types of midpoints, an up beat one and a down beat one. Which one is yours? Did you choose the right one? Does it mirror the low point?

Not Delivering on the Promise of Your Premise

One other issue that can derail Act Two of a first draft is a failure to deliver on "the promise of the premise" that you set up in Act One. Blake Snyder uses "the promise of the premise" phrase to describe the screenplay beat he calls "Fun and Games," at the beginning of Act Two. These scenes are often set pieces designed to give the audience what they want. They fulfill the genre or story expectations you have set up in Act One.

José Silerio, a screenwriter who served as Blake Snyder's development director, says the following about the promise of the premise when describing two very different films that deliver on what they promise, Roland Emmerich's action movie 2012 and the Coen brothers' drama A SERIOUS MAN:

> If you promise us the end of the world, then give us the end of the world. If you promise us a Midwestern Jewish man looking for answers as his life falls apart, then give us a Midwestern Jewish man looking for answers as his life falls apart.

You as the writer promised the audience something in Act One, and in Act Two you must deliver it to the audience or they will be disappointed. Act Two is the antithesis of Act One, remember; the audience will use it as a reference point as the story moves into Act Two. If you don't understand this, your story can lose focus because you are not delivering on the promise you made in Act One. This promised premise, of course, should keep paying off until the very end of your story, if you want to create a truly satisfying screenplay.

Common Act Three Problems

Most Act Three problems can trace their roots back to issues in Act One or Act Two. If you don't set up the story well in the first act, the audience won't have a strong sense of hope for the hero to succeed and sufficient fear that they won't by the time you get to Act Three. If you fail to build up the tension in Act Two, through ever increasing obstacles, complications and conflict with the forces of antagonism, the audience won't be invested in the outcome of the story. If you lose the plot thread, or fail to develop the character through a believable arc (change and growth), the audience will either be lost by Act Three, or not care about the protagonist enough to care what happens to them. There are a few problems that are unique to Act Three, however, and they all basically have to do with the ending of the film: does it feel real or does it feel phony?

The Unsatisfying Ending

This problem is often reduced to an argument over happy endings. Hollywood, which is in the business of making money from movies, almost demands a happy ending for its films. It's hard to sell an unhappy ending to audiences. The problem with happy endings isn't that they're happy, though, it's that they sometimes don't feel authentic or justified. A happy ending is just an ending in which the hero accomplishes his goal, and it only works if it's believable. If the hero hasn't earned his or her victory, the audience will feel dissatisfied with the ending. They will feel like it's been tacked on just to sell the movie.

An ending won't feel authentic unless if it has been properly set up. Remedying this will require you to go back to Act One and Act Two to fix the problem. One of the more classic and satisfying endings is the one in THE USUAL SUSPECTS. When a certain character (no spoilers here) turns out to be the mastermind of the whole caper, at first the audience is shocked. But then the writer and filmmaker walk us back through the story, in a series of quick flashbacks, and suddenly it all makes sense.

The Deus Ex Machina Ending

Another problem that can result in an unsatisfying ending is what is commonly called a *deus ex machina* ending. The phrase literally translates to *god from the machine*, and was a convention of Greek tragedy, where a machine was literally used to bring actors playing gods onto the stage. The concept was used to resolve the conflict and conclude the story. Its function was to resolve an otherwise irresolvable plot situation, to surprise the audience, or bring the tale to a happy ending.

The term now has a very negative connotation as a cheap plot device by which the hero's problem (their journey or quest) is resolved through the intervention of some new twist of fate, event, or character (by god, from the machine). You want to avoid this type of ending at all costs. It is the most unsatisfying ending of all, because in an ending like this the hero doesn't solve their own problem, or achieve their goal through their own struggle and efforts. Instead victory is handed to them. That will never do in modern storytelling.

A classic example of how to play with this type of *deus ex machina* ending occurs in GET OUT. At the end of the film, it looks like it's curtains for Chris, when Rose and her "mind slaves" Georgina and Walter halt his attempt to flee. As Rose is about to finish Chris off with a shotgun, Walter asks for the gun so he can kill Chris. Chris, in desperation awakens Walter with his phone flash, and instead of shooting Chris, Walter shoots Rose. For a moment, it feels like Chris's problem has been solved by Walter. Then, in a surprising twist, Walter shoots himself and Rose shows signs of life crawling desperately for the shotgun. She and Chris struggle for the weapon and Chris finally strangles Rose to death (or at least until she's no longer conscious). Chris finally defeats Rose and her cohorts, on his own, through his own actions. Only then does Rod arrive in a TSA car, and he and Chris drive safely away. Ultimately, there is no *deus ex machina* ending here. Instead, through a series of great twists and turns, Peel crafted the kind of satisfying, "happy" ending the audience was craving and that helped make the film a huge success.

Eliminating Repeated Beats

In screenwriting and in filmmaking, you don't have the luxury of repeating yourself. It's too time-consuming and too costly. From a storytelling perspective, repeating the same story beat is detrimental, because it slows your story down. If you repeat the same emotional beat, especially within a scene, but even in a sequence or a story, it's likely that you will begin to frustrate and bore the audience. "*We get it,*" they'll say. "*Move on!*" The best scenes are crucial, consequential and necessary, according to writer Erik Bork, because something happens in them that forever changes the game from that point forward. When that new thing happens, it leads to new actions, new decisions, and new circumstances for the characters, unlike what they've experienced before.

There is no need then to repeat beats. Bork points out that writers sometimes try to keep the story moving by having the protagonist take an approach to the problem/goal which fails, and then take another approach that also fails, and then another that similarly fails again. This results in an episodic narrative, not a dramatic one. The momentum stagnates, the rising action flattens, and the story suffers. Most scenes or sequences shouldn't end with the main character right back where they started. If they do, it's what Bork calls a "stutter step." This kind of scene adds nothing to the overall story. If in your script, you notice two scenes that are making the same basic story or emotional beat, you should cut one of them in your rewrite. The pace of your story will improve immediately.

Clichés and How to Avoid Them

Every genre has its clichés, its stock characters, and stereotypes. The real problem with clichés, as novelist Peter Seglin, author of *179 Ways to Save Your Novel*, says, is that they deprive your story of genuine details, which are both more convincing and more interesting than clichés. To combat cliché in your writing, try some of the following suggestions:

- *Don't Be Derivative*: Don't borrow someone else's style as your own, it will not feel authentic. Don't borrow scenes from your favorite films, create your own.
- *Avoid the Obvious*: Just because you've seen it work before, steer away from the convenient, quick solution. It's human nature to look for the obvious, but it's lazy writing. Create something unique. Put a twist on the genre movie you're writing. Look for interesting settings for scenes and stories, ones you haven't seen before.
- *Elevate the Ordinary*: One way to craft more authentic scenes is to put the focus on the everyday, ordinary concerns of your characters. Check out SNOW WHITE for a great example of this. Notice how ordinary, everyday concerns like housecleaning, dinner time preparations, and every day work are used as the foundation for creating highly entertaining scenes in a masterpiece of filmmaking.
- *Eschew Gratuitous, Melodramatic Action*: Avoid melodrama, the use of the sensational and overtly emotional at the expense of detailed characterization. Especially avoid the tendency to resort to over the top action, gratuitous violence, and phony histrionics.
- *Slow Down*: Don't rush through scenes. Take the time to fill your scenes with genuine, specific moments and details that enhance the drama or comedy in the scene. From specific details, general themes can also emerge (again see

SNOW WHITE). Once you've created a scene that feels authentic, you can then focus on trimming it, using the *get in late get out early* method.

- *Focus on Substance and Authenticity*: Don't fill your scenes with generic or gratuitous action that we've seen a million times. Focus on the reality of the situation and the truth of the characters. How would real people respond in the specific situation you've set up in the scene?

One scene that does all these things well is the classic *"I'll have what she's having"* scene in WHEN HARRY MET SALLY. The scene is a unique take on the age-old battle of the sexes. It focuses on the ordinary—two friends having lunch—and uses that ordinary setting in a unique way by having Harry and Sally play out a genuinely funny, yet personal and specific moment in front of an audience of lunchtime diners. The writing avoids melodrama by keeping Sally's re-enactment of a fake orgasm authentic, and by avoiding gratuitous, "dirty" language which would feel false for the characters. (Note that cursing is not something that you have to avoid. People swear all the time in real life. You just need to make sure it feels authentic to the characters and setting. Watch MIDNIGHT RUN or PULP FICTION to see what authentic profane dialogue sounds like).

Addressing Character Problems

Some writers are great at creating a tight, slick storyline, but have trouble with creating well-rounded, believable, unique characters. They hit all the right story beats, but the script doesn't excite readers because they aren't connecting with the characters. Character problems can fall into several major categories, starting with the hero and villain, and then the supporting characters, as discussed in the following:

Weak Protagonist

If you're getting notes about the main character in your script feeling cliché or dull, or if you're getting feedback that says readers don't seem to care what happens to them, ask yourself a few questions:

- *Is your protagonist likeable or watchable?*
  You can fix this quickly by writing a "save the cat" scene to help connect the audience to the hero, if you don't have one already. If you already have a scene like that, ask yourself if it feels cliché or inauthentic. If you're working on an antihero type as your protagonist, have you made them watchable? Look for scenes in which you can add twists to the character to surprise the reader and make them interested in following the antihero's story.

- *Is your protagonist acting or just reacting?*

  A passive hero is a dull hero. Ideally you should have addressed this issue in the structuring stage, but sometimes we drift away from our outlines as we're writing our first draft. As you look over your first draft, make sure your hero is actively doing things to achieve their goal, and not just reacting to all the obstacles you're putting in their way.

- *Is your protagonist highly motivated?*

  Sometimes, the easiest way to make the audience care what happens to the hero is to set the stakes higher. This will increase the level of hope and fear in your audience, as well as help you focus the hero's behavior in all the scenes of your script.

- *Are you communicating your protagonist's character flaw clearly?*

  Rewrite a scene or two in the first act to make the flaw more obvious to the audience, or more interesting or believable. Make sure you balance the character's flaw with likeable qualities, as the writers of DALLAS BUYERS CLUB do with their very flawed hero, Ron Woodruff.

- *Does the hero have too many flaws?*

  If people are confused by your protagonist's actions, focus in on one flaw, and eliminate or rewrite any scenes that muddle this issue. Is it clear what the hero needs to do to resolve their inner need?

Weak Antagonist

What about the villain? Ask yourself if your antagonist is as well-drawn as your hero. A well-defined antagonist will have a goal in sharp opposition to the protagonist. Look at DALLAS BUYERS CLUB, which has a great antagonist in FDA inspector Richard Barkley. Barkley doesn't want AIDS drugs being served out willy-nilly by any old joe. He wants, demands in fact, a well-regulated system, and this goes completely counter to Ron's desire to get his hands on whatever AIDS drug he thinks might benefit him or his clients. Their ever-increasing conflict over this single issue helps drive the second act story toward the climax. See if you can improve your antagonist.

Clichéd Characters

When it comes to characters, you want them to feel fresh and original, even the minor ones. One way is to find the unexpected in their personality and behavior. Ask yourself if you have seen this character before? What is different or unique about them? LEGALLY BLONDE and RAIDERS OF THE LOST ARK are full of interesting, unique, well-drawn supporting characters. A great example is Paulette, Elle's manicurist. She's quirky, funny, and incredibly sympathetic. Sallah in RAIDERS is another well-drawn supporting character.

Also remember the adage *complex characters, simple stories*. Complex doesn't mean inscrutable, it often just means a character who occasionally surprises the audience, is unique in some way, and who behaves realistically, like a human being would. Sapito, Indy's guide in the opening scene of RAIDERS, is a complex, fascinating, supporting character who is so well-drawn and believable that he has become iconic in his own right. One way to create great characters like this is to write and rewrite and polish their dialogue until it sounds unique and authentic ("*Throw me the whip, I throw you the idol!*").

Addressing Dialogue Issues

If you are like most writers, the dialogue in the first draft of your script will almost always be terrible. There are very few writers who can just drop great dialogue on the page the first time through a script. For one, most writers work quickly to knock out a first draft because they know they will be going back to rewrite it anyway. They don't sweat over every word the first time through. There will be plenty of time for that kind of hard, slow, painful work later, in the rewrite phase.

First draft dialogue is also usually bad because you as a writer are still learning who your characters are, and how they speak. Often in a first draft the characters will all sound the same, too, and more than likely they will sound like you, the writer. You want all your characters to have distinct voices, and unless you are one of the few dialogue savants out there, it will take time and many drafts to get that to happen.

There's a few simple fixes to all this dialogue trouble, and it starts with the idea that less is more. Keep your dialogue short, wherever possible. There will always be exceptions, like Quint's long multi-page monologue about the fate of the USS Indianapolis in JAWS, or the NSA speech in GOOD WILL HUNTING, but as a rule, less is more in dialogue writing just as it is in writing good action and description.

On the Nose Dialogue

If there's a cardinal sin in writing dialogue, it's what is referred to in Hollywood as "on the nose" dialogue. If someone tells you the dialogue in your screenplay is too **on the nose**, it means that the characters are saying exactly what they're thinking and feeling in too straightforward a manner. The dialogue has no subtlety or nuance, no personality. What you hear from the characters is all you get, there's no **subtext** behind the text, no inner psychology trying to work its way out.

One way to improve on the nose dialogue is to realize how often people in the real world don't say what they mean. They don't ask for what they want exactly, they don't tell you that your butt looks big in those jeans. They obfuscate, beat around the bush, and sometimes just outright tell lies. But they rarely say exactly what it is they mean. Their dialogue reflects where they grew up, how educated they are, what field of work they are in. In short, their dialogue reflects who they are. Here's a good example, again from DALLAS BUYERS CLUB:

```
INT. DALLAS MERCY HOSPITAL - ROOM - DAY 13

Ron, head and eyes bandaged, lays on a bed. After
a few beats, he peels off the eye bandages, gets
up. He opens a cabinet, then a drawer. Finds a
bag of sucking CANDY, pops a piece in his mouth,
puts some in his pocket. He sees his jacket on
the back of the door, searches his pockets for a
cigarette. He's about to light one when Dr. Sevard
enters with Eve Saks. Both wear surgical masks and
latex gloves.

                    DR. SEVARD
          Mr. Woodroof. I'm Dr. Sevard.

Ron turns to Eve, flashes a smile.

                    DR. SEVARD
          We saw something that concerned
          us in your initial blood work so
          we ran some additional tests.

                    EVE
          Blood tests.

Ron stops moving and tries to assess the situation.
Is he in trouble?

                    RON
          What kinda blood tests, cause I
          don't Use drugs.

                    EVE
          We didn't test you for drugs.
```

                    RON
          Good, cause that ain't none of
          yer business anyway.

                    DR. SEVARD
          You've tested positive for HIV --

Ron looks at Dr. Sevard blankly.

                    DR. SEVARD
          ...the virus that causes AIDS.

Ron freezes. A long beat.

                    RON
          Who you kidding, Rock cock suck-
          ing Hudson bullshit?!

                    DR. SEVARD
          Have you ever used intravenous
          drugs Or had any homosexual --

Ron spits out his CANDY.

                    RON
          Homo? Homo? That's what you
          said, right? Shit. You gotta be
          kidding me.
                    (laughs)
          I ain't no faggot, I don't even
          know any faggots, I'm a rodeo!

The room is silent.

                    RON
          Look at me, doc. Come on now,
          look At me. What do you see?

                    DR. SEVARD
          Your T-cell count is down to
          nine, A healthy person has five
          hundred To fifteen hundred.

                    RON
          What the fuck's a three-Cell?!

                    DR. SEVARD
             T-cell. Frankly we're surprised
             you're alive.

                    RON
             Well surprise this: you've made
             a fuckin' mistake!

Ron looks back and forth from Dr. Saks to Sevard.
No mistake.

                    RON
             You must've mixed my blood with
             some daisy puller or sumptin.

                    EVE
             We ran the blood test several
             times.

Eve hands him some pamphlets and other paper
work.

                    EVE
             That's some information on HIV
             and AIDS you may find informa-
             tive and your test results.

Ron flips through the papers. Becomes frustrated by
terminology he doesn't understand.

                    DR. SEVARD
             Mr. Woodroof, we're trying to
             impress upon you the gravity of
             your situation.

Based on your condition, we estimate that you
have about thirty days to get your affairs in
order --

                    RON
             Thirty days?

Ron jumps off the examining table.

                    RON
             What is this shit?!

They don't respond.

Ron laughs incredulously and walks towards the
door.

```
            RON
I got a news flash for all
y'all, There ain't nothin' out
there that can kill Ron Woodroof
in thirty days.

Ron looks at the papers, tosses them up in the
air and exits.
```

You hear this dialogue and you know a lot about who all the characters in this scene are, their jobs, their level of education, their values and beliefs.

Moving Beyond Structure

There's an old theater adage that says, *if it's not on the page, it's not on the stage.* For the most part, this is true for screenplays and movies, too. A great screenplay almost never results in a bad movie. But plenty of bad movies, too many to count, are the direct result of bad screenplays. The blueprint stunk, and so did the final product. So, what can a screenwriter do to avoid this most obvious pitfall? The answer: pay attention to the details. Get them right.

Format

Formatting is one such detail that is important to the finished product, as we mentioned in the last chapter. Your script should look like a standard movie script if you want people in the industry to take it seriously. It's a minor, but important detail. Another example of knowing which details are important and which aren't can be found in many first-time writers' first scripts. Novice writers, both young and old, think they must describe every camera move in their story, but forget to describe their main characters with even a little bit of useful information. One detail, camera moves, is completely unnecessary. Camera movement is the director's job, so don't waste precious script real estate laying down detailed moves. Most directors will ignore them at best. It's like telling a builder how to saw a piece of wood. The other detail, describing a character, is much more crucial—it's telling the builder what kind of wood to use. Here's a few more details to pay attention to in the writing phase.

Writing Visually

Film is fundamentally a visual medium, unlike the novel which is fundamentally text based. Meaning is conveyed in movies visually, with some deference to sound (dialogue and music for the most part). When you write a script, it's important to remember this, and to write visually. What does writing visually mean? Well, it might be more instructive to state first what it isn't. It's not putting more words on paper, or lots and lots of description. It's not adding more dialogue that tells the reader what the character is seeing or doing. It's also, as we've said, not including camera movements or angles, which are the director's turf.

Writing visually is about being very selective in your choice of words, and using as few as words as possible, to paint pictures in the heads of your audience. Make them see the movie from the words you've written on the page. Screenwriting is saying the most with the fewest words possible. That includes your description and dialogue. Note that, if you use too many words, what they'll see is a bunch of text on the page. Too much text, too many words, will overwhelm the visual images you are trying to create. Action and description in screenplays is best conveyed through simple, clear, short phrases.

Screenwriters today are always looking for new ways to write description that grabs the reader's attention. When describing action, short bursts of words with a minimal but judicious use of adjectives is a good way to go. Look at the example below from NIGHTCRAWLER, screenplay by Dan Gilroy. Notice the brevity with which Gilroy shows us what's important in the scene:

```
DEAD OF NIGHT

as LOU drives an empty valley boulevard ...
holding his

CELL PHONE

on the steering wheel ... surfing a SEX
HOOK-UP WEBSITE as

PHOTOS OF NEAR NAKED WOMEN

with their locations are shown ... LOU stops
scrolling on

A WOMAN

in her 40s, semi-clothed and

LOU

turns the phone... snaps a smiling self-
portrait and CUT TO
```

Here's a good example of visual description, using standard screenplay format, from opening scene of THE SECRET LIFE OF WALTER MITTY:

```
INT. WALTER'S APARTMENT, BROOKLYN - MORNING

Walter Mitty (30s) sits at his small kitchen table,
balancing his check book. We see his last several
expense entries:

Mom's new apt. deposit

eHarmony sign-up

O's braces (2nd installment)

Piano movers

Piano storage

Piano delivery to Mom's new apt.

In-piano humidity control system

EXT. CORNER 5TH AVENUE, 43RD STREET, NYC - DAY

During the morning rush hour, a crowd of business-
men waits on the corner to cross the street. Walter
is among them, dressed in a short-sleeve business
shirt and tie and with a briefcase on hand. Nothing
happens. Then Walter's head explodes.

CREDITS BEGIN

Up toward the clouds, propelled skyward, were the
contents (ideas and images) of Walter's head;
they've begun to float toward the ground.
```

Note how simple the description is, and how judiciously writer Steve Conrad picks and chooses what to show you, the reader. It takes only a few words, and we begin to see who Walter is, and what his problem is too (a mundane life that is constricting a wild imagination).

Choose words that evoke images. Using colors is a great way to evoke visuals images with a minimal number of words. You can write the word *truck*, and it conveys a generic image. Write *red truck*, though and you've created a more specific, more visual image. Also choose adjectives, and adverbs, that are visual and specific. For example, instead of just saying *truck*, say a *rusty, red pickup truck.* That image forms quickly in the mind. When describing action, short bursts of words with a minimal but judicious use of adjectives is a good way to go. For example:

```
EXT. DALLAS MERCY HOSPITAL - REAR - DAY 31

A steady drizzle. Ron stands out by the dumpster,
his boots and cowboy hat soaked. The Hispanic
Orderly emerges from the hospital, a large gar-
bage bag in his hands.

                    HISPANIC ORDERLY
              There ain't no more, they
              started lockin' it up.

The Orderly throws the garbage into the dumpster.

                    RON
              I got more cash.

The Orderly studies Ron who holds out some money.
The Orderly snatches it, and writes something on
a piece of paper.

                    ORDERLY
              Here. In Mexico. A doctor, he
              has some.

Ron takes the paper, looks at it.

                    RON
              What the hell is this bullshit?

Ron takes a swing at the Orderly but misses.
Something about Ron is off. We hear the ringing
sound again. Ron struggles to stand and collapses
onto the ground. Black.
```

There are several types of description that are important: *character appearance, location appearance,* and *important objects or sounds.* Keep your descriptions short, and make sure they illicit images in the reader's mind. For example:

```
INT. DALLAS MERCY HOSPITAL - DR. EVE SAKS'
OFFICE - DAY 21

Diplomas hang in neat rows. A perfectly ordered
desk. Eve meticulously records numbers on a chart.
```

```
                    RON (O.S.)
          Can you get me AZT?

Eve looks up as Ron walks in and sits down.

                    RON
          Barrow Wilkem just released it
          for testing, right? This hospi-
          tal is one of the sites.

She nods yes, surprised how well informed he is.

                    RON
          Well can I buy some?
```

Handling Exposition

Exposition can be another tricky thing to write, because it's technically not action or description, but information that the audience needs to follow the story. Every script needs some exposition, to help give context to the story and the characters, but most first drafts contain far too much of it. One way to hide exposition is to cover it through humor. The recent film THE MARTIAN is a good example of how to do this. The film is a science fiction movie, and full of exposition that is necessary for the audience to understand the science behind the story. To make this palatable to a general audience, the writer has the main character deliver exposition throughout the film in various humorous ways. THE BIG SHORT is a brilliant example of how to use humor to deliver exposition, going so far as to have actress Margot Robbie explain derivates and credit default swaps while enjoying a bubble bath.

Michael Schilf, co-founder of *The Script Lab*, lists five handy tools for writing exposition into your screenplay:

1. Eliminate exposition that isn't absolutely necessary.
2. Deliver exposition through conflict.
3. Wait as long as possible before providing exposition, always looking for the moment of maximum dramatic impact to reveal it.
4. Use brevity. Just give the necessary information, and move forward.
5. Use a character (main or supporting) whose job it is to deliver exposition: a judge, teacher, military officer, principle, politician, scientist, and so on.

The key with exposition is to deliver it in a way that doesn't kill the pace of the story. A great example of how to cleverly deliver exposition while maintaining pace is the Army Intelligence scene in the first act of RAIDERS. The whole scene is in fact expository, laying out all the important information the audience needs to understand what the Ark of the Covenant is, and why it's important, but doing so in an entertaining, visual way.

Developing the Theme

One more thing you can do to improve your first draft is to develop the theme in your script. Theme, remember, is what Lajos Egri focused on as the key to creating a strong premise for your movie. *Stinginess leads to ruin, pride goeth before the fall, slow and steady wins the race* are all examples of classic themes in storytelling. There are many ways to evaluate the theme of a screenplay.

One way is to look at how theme and character connect, as writing guru Chuck Wendig explains: "The protagonist is at odds with the theme and rails against it, eventually overcoming it, overturning it, or succumbing to it and proving it out." DALLAS BUYERS CLUB is a perfect illustration of a hero succumbing to a theme and proving it out, the theme in this case being, we're all human and deserve to be loved.

As you rewrite your script, think about what the theme of your story is. Ask yourself if there's a scene in the film where you can state the theme. This is best done in the first act, and usually best delivered in dialogue by someone other than the main character. Look at each scene in your script and think about ways to rewrite that scene that reinforce the theme. Don't repeat the same point over and over again in similar ways, however. Look for unique ways to show the theme at play, rather than having a character repeat it in dialogue.

Polishing the Script

Once you've rewritten the script, and perhaps rewritten it many times, you'll come to the final stage of the writing process—the polish. In this phase, you won't be changing much if anything at all that you've written. You'll first look for any typos or formatting errors and fix those. Then you should look over your scenes one more time to see if any repeat story beats, and consider cutting those.

Kill Your Darlings

At this stage, and even sooner, the screenwriting truism of **killing your darlings** will come into play. Killing your darlings means eliminating every single moment, beat, or scene that does not serve a purpose in the story, or that repeats a story beat or an emotional beat that exists in an earlier scene. You must cut those scenes or parts of scenes out, no matter how much you love them. You must kill those darlings to make your script as tight as possible. Think of each word, each line of your script as costing you money. Then try to save as much money as you can by eliminating waste. You must take off your writer's hat and put on the editor's cap here, and be ruthless in this stage.

The Title

One last thing to do before you finish, is to make sure your title is really good. In Hollywood, this is important, because the title is the first thing agents, producers, and studio executives will see when they open up your script to read. If the title is catchy, clever, or intriguing, it will make them want to turn the page. A great title will be brief, and often two words are best, three at most. It may hint at the central conflict in the story (THE EXORCIST). A great title may also reflect the theme (ORDINARY PEOPLE), the genre (LEGALLY BLONDE, which sounds funny and so tells the audience to expect to laugh), the hero (LAWRENCE OF ARABIA) or the villain (ALIEN). It might relate to a memorable line from the story (TO KILL A MOCKINGBIRD). The thing to remember with the title is that in Hollywood, and in screenwriting in general, titles matter, so spend some time working on it, rewriting and polishing it to make is as good as the script that follows it.

Example: First Draft and Rewrite of a Scene

Below is an actual scene written by an undergraduate student and first-time screenwriter. This young student had developed their story, THE ROAD LESS TRAVELLED, using the same process we've described in Part One of this book. They started with a logline: *An adventurous, bored girl is forced to choose between staying in the town she's lived all her life or traveling the world with a mysterious musician she just met when her boyfriend asks her to marry him.* The writer worked out the acts, and the beats, and when it came time to start writing, this was the first draft of the opening scene that they turned in:

```
EXT. SUMMER OLD TOWN, NIGHT

Girl driving around in truck blaring music down a
country road. Credits are rolling as she's driv-
ing around this old town. She stops and comes up
to build. She climbs on top of the car and gets
to roof.

                    EMMA
              Hello beautiful
```

```
She stares out to the perfect night skyline.
She then pulls out her iPod. Sound of silence by
Simon and Garfunkel

                    EMMA
            One day.... one day...

Police shouts out of car.

                    POLICE
            HEY WHAT ARE YOU DOING UP
            THERE!?

Credits roll of her driving around running away
from the police. She ends driving back to her house
and cuts the lights off.

Fade to black
```

As you can see, this is very much a first draft of a scene. It's very rough, and looks and reads like it was written rather quickly (which it was). After working in class on analyzing what could be improved in the rewrite, and covering all the items we've mentioned in this chapter so far, this student went home, a little down, but ready and willing to tackle a rewrite. They followed up a couple weeks later with the following second draft:

```
EXT. ROOFTOP - NIGHT

EMMA (19) sits on top of roof of old abandoned
movie theater. She's reading a letter she got
from New York University with a half of a six-pack
gone. Tear stains down the rejection letter.

                    EMMA
            Dear Ms. Emma Morgan we are
            sorry to inform you that we
            couldn't accept you into our
            music program this semester.

She stares at a highway sign. It reads "New York
142 miles". She continues to drink.

                    EMMA
            God isn't this just perfect.
            That was my way out......I was
            so close.
```

She stares out at the sign. The highway is so close. She realizes how far her dreams are away and throws a beer bottle at sign.

Beer bottle is launched and hits police officer DAN's car.

DAN (23) is a new police officer recently hired by Emma's dad.

> DAN
> OH MY GOD WHAT WAS THAT.

Emma looks down at cop car

> EMMA
> Shit.

Sees Dan take a gun out and nervously search around his car and everywhere else to see what's going on.

> DAN
> I am warning you.... Please come out with your hands up.

> EMMA
> Shit shit shit shit. I'll just hideHere. maybe he will go away.

> DAN
> Who's up there? Stay right there don't you move.

EMMA frantically cleans up beer and runs for the stairs for the door. As soon as she opens up the door DAN is there.

> EMMA
> Shit.

> DAN
> Shit.

They awkwardly stand there both trying to figure out whatto do next.

                              DAN
            Emma... what are you doing up
            here?

                              EMMA
            Enjoying the view as I always
            do. Hey want a beer? ha ha oh
            no....

                              DAN
            Emma! What are you doing with
            beer? You aren't old enough.

                              EMMA
            Come on Dan I'm almost old
            enough.

                              DAN
            I can't. What if your dad finds
            out I let you drink.

                              EMMA
            He doesn't have to know!

     Dan stands there unsure then makes his decision.

                              DAN
            That's it I have an idea!

This second draft of the scene is an obvious improvement. The student added conflict and improved the dialogue, made the protagonist more interesting, and even improved the action and description. That's no small achievement for a first-time screenwriter. This scene still has issues that should be addressed, however. It would need to be rewritten several more times to be really good, and that's the point. Good writing requires rewriting. Jordan Peele, who won the Academy Award for Best Screenplay in 2018 for his screenplay for GET OUT, says he did 37 drafts of his script before it was filmed. He may have been the first African-American to win the Oscar for best screenplay, but he's not the first successful screenwriter to rewrite their script dozens of times. Rewriting is the nature of the beast, and an indispensable part of the screenwriting process. If you want to be a successful screenwriter, you won't skip it. In fact, you'll embrace it, and make it a part of your normal writing life. And your work will be all the better for it.

EXERCISES

Exercise 1: Rewrite the following first draft of this scene from the student script THE ROAD LESS TRAVELED. Work on improving the action, description, and dialogue. Focus on improving conflict in the scene. See if you can find a way to emotionally connect the audience to the protagonist. Correct any screenplay formatting errors or typos you find as well.

```
EXT. SUMMER IN AN OLD SMALL TOWN, DAY

Emma is wearing a black shirt, ripped jeans long
black hair and has this rebellious look to her.
Brock is wearing ripped jeans and a sleeveless t
shirt. Emma is listening to her music while Brock
is trying to have a conversation.

                    BROCK
          So I heard you snuck out again.

                    EMMA
          *ignoring him*

                    BROCK
          Excuse me? Are you listen-
          ing to me?

                    EMMA
          * turns music up even more*

                    BROCK
          Seriously you and your stupid
          music (pulls headphones off her)

                    EMMA
          Seriously what could you want?

                    BROCK
          You are sneaking around at night
          again! Are you cheating on me?

                    EMMA
          Brock...(sarcaticallY) Brocky
          Boo why would I cheat on you?
          Maybe I want to have a little
          more fun in this dull town.
```

                    BROCK
          Seriously theres more to this
          town then you think Emma!

                    EMMA
          Oh really? Like what? Everything
          must be so hard for the towns
          star quarterback who won them 3
          high school championships OH MY
          GOD.

                    BROCK
          Actually it was only 2...

                    EMMA
          Holy shit who cares?? Seriously
          no one. There are people out
          there living life in the now not
          in the past.

                    BROCK
          Whatever Emma you know you are
          really something else you have
          it great here. You are dating
          the towns celebrity, you have a
          great job at the radio station
          and life could be way worse.

                    EMMA
          Sometimes I wish I didnt have
          it so grea. Sometimes I wish my
          life was different.

                    BROCK
          Oh good Im glad you wish that.
          After all I have given you?

                    EMMA
          Oh here we go.

                    BROCK
          Who got you the job at the radio
          station? Who has been taking care
          of you since your parents left
          when we were 15? Hmm oh yeah MR.
          "no one cares about your past"

                    EMMA
          look im sorry

                    BROCK
          No you arent... You just think
          everythings sooo bad. Come on I
          can be fun.

                    EMMA
          You seriously took me to our
          high school football game so
          everyone can kiss your ass.

                    BROCK
          That was not the reason It was
          fun! Besides we saw all our
          favorite teachers.

                    EMMA
          Yes seeing MRS. O'Malley again
          its great knowing the crypt
          keeper is still around.

                    BROCK
          Listen you better change your
          attitude or we are through. Im
          so sick of you being like this.
          So get it together or no more
          Brocky Boo.

Exercise 2: Now looking over this rewrite, and explain what you changed and why? How do you think you improved this scene?

Exercise 3: Rewrite the opening and then the first act of your script.

Exercise 4: Rewrite and polish your entire script.

FURTHER READINGS:

On Writing by Stephen King

Your Screenplay Sucks by William Akers

Rewriting Your Script: 10 Part Series by Scott Myers, available at https://gointo-thestory.blcklst.com/rewriting-your-script-10-part-series-35e1c96fdc8d

10 Tips to Avoid Clichés in Writing by Peter Seglin, available at http://www.writersdigest.com/whats-new/10-tips-to-bypass-cliche-and-melodrama

25 Things You Should Know About Antagonists by Chuck Wendig, available at http://terribleminds.com/ramble/2012/07/24/25-things-you-should-know-about-antagonists/

Flying Wrestler by Eric Bork, screenwriting blog available at www.flyingwrestler.com

David Freeman's Beyond Structure by David Freeman, available at www.beyond-structure.com

PART 3
The Real World

The Business of Screenwriting

10

Unlike other forms of writing like poetry and novels, screenplays don't serve a standalone function; screenplays wouldn't exist at all if Hollywood didn't need them. Like plays and novels, you can read scripts for entertainment. But unlike plays and novels, scripts are not usually packaged and sold on their own, and only then if the script led to a successfully produced film. Even today, few people go out of their way to buy screenplays just to read them.

Screenplays developed as a form and style of writing over a period of decades to facilitate the mass production of movies, because the big studios, and most filmmakers, found it easier to create films from written blueprints. The producers and studios who financed films found that written scripts made the process of making movies more efficient, and thus less costly and potentially more profitable. All this is to say that screenplays, and thus screenwriting, don't exist in a vacuum. If you want to write for writing's sake, you may want to think about being a novelist or a poet. There's a much broader market for your work in those mediums.

HOLLYWOOD FILM PRODUCTION

If you are going to be a screenwriter, you should understand how the business works. There are five basic **phases of film production** in the movie business:

- **Development:** During this phase movie producers and studios look for and/or develop material into screenplays.
- **Pre-production:** During this phase, producers look for financing and talent (actors, directors) to attach to the project. Budgeting and scheduling happen here as well.
- **Production:** In this phase, usually the briefest, the screenplay is filmed.

- **Post-production:** This is when the movie is edited and special effects, music & sound effects, and titles are added.
- **Distribution:** Films that have been completed look for distribution in the marketplace in this phase, either through the traditional routes of movie theaters and television, or newer avenues like DVD and digital streaming.

As you can see, writers are only required for the first phase, and their screenplays for the second, third, and sometimes fourth phases. It can take dozens, sometimes hundreds of people to make a movie, so you as the screenwriter are just one cog, albeit an important one, in this production machine. It's good to remember that.

The market for screenplays is small, the buyers few, comparatively speaking. According to Box Office Mojo, the number of films produced each year has hovered around 700 for the last few years. If you look back at the 1990s and early 2000s, the numbers were between 450 and 500. The trend is up because digital production technology has lowered the barriers of entry to film production, and more important perhaps, opened new distribution channels for film producers like Netflix, Amazon, and iTunes. The cold hard numerical facts aren't meant to discourage you, only to give you a realistic view of the economics of screenwriting.

STUDIOS, PRODUCERS, AND GREENLIGHTING POWER

Studios and the movie producers who work for them or have deals to produce movies with them (called **studio deals**) need screenplays for this method of production to work. This is what creates the demand for good screenwriters and good screenplays. That demand can drive up the cost of a great script by a great writer, but it also makes for a limited market for screenplays. Most producers and studio executives don't have the power to finance a film, known in the business as **greenlighting** power, either. Only studio heads, and a few others, have this power, because it entails releasing and putting at risk the millions of dollars required to produce a single Hollywood film.

On the other hand, it may only cost a few thousand dollars for a producer or studio to purchase a script. The cost to purchase a script varies widely, and depends a great deal on whether the film is being made by a studio or independently financed. The Writers Guild of America sets the minimum amounts that the major studios must pay to buy a script from a screenwriter (more on the

WGA in a moment). The rights to make a film from a script can also be sold to a producer for as little as a few hundred dollars; this is called purchasing an **option**. An option allows a producer the exclusive rights to shop a script to the big studios for a limited time period, usually 12–18 months. During this time, the producer may work with the writer to develop and polish the script, and they may also look to attach talent to the project (name actors or a director). If the studio decides to make this film, they will then purchase the script outright. This purchase deal may include attaching the producer who had the option as well as the writer, or the studio may opt to bring in another writer or producer to help get the film made.

The art of the Hollywood deal is too convoluted to describe in one chapter of a screenwriting textbook, but the long and short of all this means that there are more film scripts in the pipeline than films being made. A lot more if you consider all the scripts written by writers without deals (this kind of script is called a **spec script** in the business). Recently, studio purchases of spec scripts hovered around 120 a year. Most Hollywood movies, however, are produced from scripts based on already existing material (novels, comic books, and plays). Those scripts also need screenwriters, though, and so that is another market for screenwriters' services. Most of these films, however, are written by screenwriters with a proven track record in the business.

Assuming, that a studio invests in three scripts for every one movie it produces in a year, that means somewhere around 2,000 scripts a year earn a writer (or writers) some money when sold or **optioned** by Hollywood studios and producers. That number may fluctuate greatly from year to year, but that's the reality of the screenwriting business, and you should know it.

INDEPENDENT FILM PRODUCTION

Movies are made outside the Hollywood studio system every day by independent producers who cobble together the funds to make their films from various non-studio sources. Some of these films go on to be quite successful, either critically or at the box office. Several of the best films of the last 10 or 20 years have been independent film productions. Often these films are first released at film festivals, like Cannes, Sundance, South by Southwest, and the Toronto International Film Festival (TIFF), and sold to studios or distributors at **film markets** associated with these and a few other festivals around the world. Most independent movies made however are genre films that go **straight to video**, meaning you never see them in a movie theater. Most of these indie movies are either action or horror films.

The cost of producing a film has dropped drastically in the last 10 years or so because of the advent of digital technology, so you can shoot a film independent of studio financing on an inexpensive video camera, edit it on your computer at home, and distribute it via any number of digital platforms. Many independent filmmakers act as writers, directors, and producers of their own films, but independent film producers are always looking for good screenplays, or good source material from which to develop screenplays, so this too is a viable market for screenwriters to explore. The purchase and option prices in the independent film world vary widely and are usually much lower than prices for scripts made by Hollywood studios.

The economics and logistics of independent filmmaking are beyond the scope of this book. *The Hollywood Producers Directory* is a valuable resource guide to the marketplace for scripts. This book is updated yearly and includes a comprehensive list of independent and studio-based producers, studios, and studio executives working in film and television production. If you want to learn more about indie film production, there are several excellent books on the subject. First and foremost is the book *Filmmakers and Financing* by Louise Levison. This is one of the best books on independent film production, and it's worth a read if your interests lie more in independent film production than Hollywood studio based productions.

AGENTS, MANAGERS, AND LAWYERS

Because there is real money out there for selling a screenplay, middlemen have found their way into the process. These middlemen act as brokers between the studios (and the producers affiliated with them) and screenwriters. There are three types: agents, managers, and lawyers. Lawyers, because they must pass a state bar exam and adhere to a code of professional ethics or be disbarred, are the easiest to deal with directly. A reputable studio or producer will not look at unsolicited material from a writer they don't know personally. Screenwriters can pay entertainment attorneys who specialize in the film business to represent their scripts to these producers and studios. Most lawyers don't usually have much cache in the business, but they are ethical and reliable, and will provide this service for an hourly or flat fee.

Agents, as Stephanie Palmer of the website *Good In A Room* defines them, are "brokers. [I]n the same way stockbrokers buy and sell stock and are paid on commission, screenplay agents broker transactions between buyers and sellers and are paid only when the deals go through. So, when an agent reads a script for the first time, they think: 'How am I going to sell this?'" Agents will usually take 10% of any script sale they make. They are always on the prowl to make sales, and the easier that sale is for them, the happier they are. According to Palmer, there are seven things all agents look for in screenplays:

1. **[A] terrific role for a movie star ("actor bait")**
2. **The project fits easily in [a] genre**
   When reading a script, a screenplay agent's question about genre is, *"Will this meet the audience's expectations for this genre?"*
3. **Super short pitch**
   Your short pitch is 1–3 sentences that encapsulates the main idea clearly and concisely. Typically, this is a "selling" logline of your project that communicates the main idea.
4. **Reading the script is not required**
   After simply hearing the short pitch [*your logline*] and reading **coverage** provided by someone, the agent trusts that if the storyline is clear and easily understood, the agent can sell your script. [*Coverage is typically done by a paid* **script reader**.]
5. **Polished script**
   Agents have short attention spans (like most people in Hollywood) and so you want to capitalize on their enthusiasm right away. Some screenplay agents give excellent notes and are skilled with script development, but most are not.
6. **Project could be made "for a price"**
   The lower the budget for the production is, the more potential buyers there are for each script. Unfortunately, there are only a handful of buyers who are able to finance big budget fare which makes the odds of selling that much more challenging.
7. **Potential for additional sales embedded in project**
   Screenplay agents know that the best time to make a sale is right after the first sale. This way they can capitalize and very likely sell your second script for more than they sold your first script—provided the scripts are in the same genre.

Top agents LOVE to hear that you have multiple projects in the same genre (rather than having scripts in a bunch of different genres). And if there is a sequel or spin-off potential in your project, that can warm the cockles of a screenwriting agent's heart.

Agents who operate in California must be licensed by the state. There are a few literary agents based in New York or elsewhere outside Hollywood who handle screenplays, but as a screenwriter you should only be concerned with the ones who are based in Los Angeles, as those are the ones who know the film business and the players best.

It's very difficult for a young or first-time screenwriter to get an agent. Agents don't normally have the time or inclination to nurture young screenwriters or develop scripts. They won't normally even read spec scripts from unproven writers. None of the big agencies will accept unsolicited screenplays (for liability reasons). As a novice writer, only a referral by someone the agent knows and trusts will likely get them to look at your script.

Smaller agencies have their own script submission policies. You should query an agent in writing before you send a script to them asking for representation. Big or small, most agents won't usually be the ones who read your script. That job will fall to a junior agent or more likely a **script reader**, who will do **coverage** on the script. This coverage is a one- or two-page summary of the script highlighting its strengths and weaknesses. Senior agents read that coverage, and then decide if your script is something they might consider representing.

Managers, unlike agents, are prohibited by California law from directly negotiating contracts for clients. By law, agents must work out of an office, but managers can work from wherever they please. Agents cannot act as producers of their own clients' projects, but managers can and often do. Managers also will take the time to nurture writing clients. For that reason, they take on fewer writers and spend more time helping them develop scripts. They also can take a higher percentage of any sale, usually getting between 10% and 15%. Because managers cannot legally make sales or negotiate contracts for writers, any writer with only a manager representing them must also have a lawyer (or agent) to handle any sales. As a service to all writers (members and non-members), the Writers Guild of America, West provides an online list of all licensed, signatory agents and agencies who represent film, television, and interactive writers.

THE WRITERS' GUILD OF AMERICA, EAST AND WEST

All screenwriters should know about the Writers Guild of America, East and West, (WGAE if you live east of the Mississippi, and WGAW if you live west of it). The Writers Guild is the labor union that represents professional writers of television, film, and increasingly of digital media content as well. WGA members write big budget films, independent movies, late night comedy/variety shows, daytime serials, broadcast and radio news, web series, documentaries, and animation. The WGA works to promote and protect the "professional and artistic interests" of the media writing community. The Guild provides services regardless of a writers' level of success.

The WGAW, through its agreements with Hollywood studios, sets minimum purchase prices for screenplays. It also offers certain benefits and protections to its members. To become a member, you must earn a minimum number of writing credits over a three-year period for work paid for by a Guild signatory producer or studio. The details of WGA membership requirements are available here: http://www.wga.org/the-guild/going-guild/join-the-guild.

The guild will not offer you any assistance in finding an agent. If you aren't sure whether an agent or an agency is legitimate, you can contact the Guild's Agency Department at (323) 782-4502, and they will tell you if that agent or agency is licensed. It's best to only deal with agents who are licensed and regulated by the state of California. For more information on the Writers Guild, visit their website at: http://www.wga.org/the-guild/about-us/guide-to-the-guild.

COPYRIGHTING OR REGISTERING YOUR SCRIPT

Many writers are concerned about protecting their ideas against being stolen or plagiarized, and so look to copyright their work. Copyrights, however, cannot protect ideas. Obtaining a copyright for your screenplay only protects the actual script or screenplay you have written. It does not protect your general idea or concept for a movie or TV show.

All scripts, all written works in fact, have **copyright protection** as soon as they are written. The author of a work ordinarily owns the copyright, unless the work was written as part of the writer's job or the writer signed a **work for hire agreement**. By law, a copyright owner has the exclusive right to make and distribute copies of the work, prepare derivative works, and perform and display the work publicly. You don't need to place a copyright notice on your script for it to receive copyright protection, but a notice can identify the copyright owner and remind others that the work is copyrighted.

Although your script is copyrighted as soon as you write it, registration with the United States Copyright Office offers some important benefits if someone infringes your copyright. First, registration creates a public record of your copyright ownership along with the date the script was created. Second, if your work is copyrighted, you can sue someone for copyright infringement. If you register it before the infringement occurs, you can also recover additional money damages and attorney's fees if you win the case. It's best to register the copyright within five years of the work's completion as this makes it easier to prove in court that you are the owner of the copyright. A work can be copyrighted online through the U.S. Copyright Office's website for about $40. It costs about double that to copyright it via a hardcopy sent through the mail.

The WGA also offers a script registration option, which is different from a copyright. WGA registration does not carry the same legal weight as a United States copyright, but it can still be useful. By registering a script with the WGA, you can document your authorship of the material from a given date forward. Registration can provide a record of your claim to authorship of a script, treatment, synopsis or outline, which may be useful if legal action is initiated or required at any point. You do not need to be a WGAW member to use this service. You can register your script with the WGA online at https://www.wgawregistry.org/registration.asp. The fee is currently $20.

SCREENPLAY CONTESTS

Because getting an agent or manager to read your script can be very difficult, many young writers turn to screenplay contests. The hope is that by winning a contest, you will generate the necessary publicity, or **buzz**, needed to entice an agent, manager, producer, or studio executive to read your script. This can be true for some contests and for some screenplays. It's not true, however, for all contests. So which ones are worth it? Christopher Lockhart, a longtime Hollywood script reader who blogs about screenwriting on his website *The Inside Pitch*, offers the following advice on screenplay contests:

The question about screenwriting contests pops up weekly on this page. "Will screenwriting contests advance my career?" "Is this a good contest?" "Which screenwriting contests are the best?" And so on. There are a trillion screenwriting contests from which to choose, so there's no straight answer to these questions. Furthermore, writers enter contests for different reasons. One writer just might want to see if her new script is good enough to make it to a second round. Another writer might be looking for some feedback. And yet another might want to win the cash prize.

It seems like a new screenwriting contest is born every day. Many make promises or allusions to opening Hollywood doors and exposing winning scripts to greenlighters. And new screenwriters shell out entry fees, hoping a win will be their golden ticket to get inside.

To be blunt, most screenwriting contests suck and are not worth the entry fee—unless what you seek is purely intrinsic value. I don't have a problem with contests *per se*, because they are helpful in keeping writers goal-oriented, providing some adrenaline and hopeful thoughts, and maybe even boasting rights. Some contests actually shell out big prize money that can help make writing the next script a little easier.

The two best reasons to enter a contest are (1) big cash prize or (2) genuine entrée into the business. Two contests that have been effective in opening doors for writers are the Nicholl Fellowship and the Trackingb Contest. Both are very different but have better odds than others in introducing new writers to Hollywood. Writers from these contests have launched careers as a DIRECT result of the contest, and some of the winning scripts have been produced. Other contests promise similar results but don't have the stats to back it up. In addition to opening doors, the Nicholl Fellowship also has a generous cash prize (35K). Because it is a fellowship, you must complete a new script during the year. The Trackingb contest has no cash prize, an expensive entry fee, but boasts winning scripts like "Extant," which became a Steven Spielberg produced TV series with Halle Berry for CBS.

Most contests cannot boast this kind of professional pedigree—regardless of how they present themselves. Most do not have the clout or visibility level to help a writer achieve professional status. Be wary of contests that boast more dubious distinctions. "This contest got me my first agent, who introduced to me to a studio executive, who introduced me to a producer, who introduced me to a bigger agent, who sat on my script for three years forcing me to leave him and sign with a manager, who insisted I write a new script, which I sold seven years later. If it weren't for this contest, I never would have made it."

Believe it or not, that kind of testimonial would motivate a lot of writers to cut a check and send in their script.

Avoid being swayed by testimonials and look for SPECIFIC results in the criteria that matter most to you when shopping for a contest. Most contests plaster their websites with vague results like, "Jim Jones signed with a huge Hollywood manager after winning our contest." "Mary Smith sold her winning script to one of Hollywood's most prolific producers." In this town, we LOVE to drop names. When people are cryptic—it's probably bullshit. If a contest can't be forthright, don't be quick to send them your money. Use Google to search for the names of winners to see if the contest has moved the needle for them. Can't find anything? You've found plenty.

Before choosing a contest, decide upon your goal. If you merely want feedback, choose a contest that's known for providing good feedback. If you're looking for a monetary prize, choose a contest that awards a big purse, if you want to brag in a query letter about placing/winning in a contest, you need to choose one that has marquee value (which is the Nicholl Fellowship or studio fellowships). Other contests might offer prizes such as Hollywood face-to-face meetings or a reading of your script (or pages of your script). This could be fun and have some value, but take into consideration if the contest pays your way and puts you up. If you have to spend a $1000 for winning a contest, it may not be worth it. Furthermore, a lot of these meetings and script readings are more of a "cool factor" than anything significant. Like all contests they just feed the Hollywood dream. But if that's what you're in the market for, do the research to ensure the details of the win meet your expectations.

Although there are lots of pros and cons with screenwriting contests (probably more of the latter than former), my bone of contention is in the judging process. The judging in most screenwriting contests is disingenuous. Since contest judges get paid very little or nothing at all, it's absurd, generally speaking, to assume that a judge, assigned 30 scripts (as an example), will read each script cover to cover. Let's say it takes a judge 90 minutes to read a script. (It takes me two hours to read a 120-page script, but I'll speculate at a faster rate of speed.) A judge will have invested 45 hours into reading those 30 scripts. If he gets paid $10 a script, he's earned about $6.60 an hour. I guess in these hard, economic times, any salary is appreciated. But, in reality, the way to make that $10 a script fee pay-off is to reduce the amount of hours put into reading. That $6.60 an hour can easily be transformed into $13 an hour by reading the 30 scripts in half the amount of time. How is that accomplished? By simply reading the first 5 or 10 pages of each script and tossing aside the screenplays that suck. This is a reality of screenplay contests. This is the way most judging occurs. There is little to no transparency in this process. Because judging is done at home, away from contest administrators, bosses can turn a blind eye to the practice.

Ethically speaking, this is the way Hollywood itself treats scripts. Most agents or producers aren't going to read more than ten pages if they cannot connect with the material. Of course, the difference between Hollywood and screenwriting contests is that Hollywood doesn't charge the writer. Contests charge entry fees and, I suspect, some contestants believe their scripts are read from fade-in to fade-out in exchange for their money. I'd have more respect for contests if they simply described the entry fee as an administration fee that did not guarantee any script be read in its entirety. But that might turn-off potential contestants, who believe their script should be read cover-to-cover. (And I happen to agree.) This is the dirty little secret of screenwriting contests.

As far as I know, screenwriting contests are unregulated. I could start THE INSIDE PITCH SCREENWRITING CONTEST, charge a $50 entry fee, put all the scripts in a big pile and toss a puppy on top. Whichever script he pees on—WINS. There's not much more to it.

I'd say that as a script progresses toward finalist status, it's far more likely to be read from beginning to end. If a script is bumped out early— probably not. In defense of contests, can anyone say the voting process for, as an example, the Oscars or Golden Globes is done with any more integrity? The process of getting into film festivals probably isn't any better either. As a result, writers entering contests might suspect some of these indiscretions yet choose to accept them with the hopes if they win the big prize, it won't matter in the end.

Market yourself wisely after winning or placing in a contest. Often, what you perceive to be a crowning achievement is meaningless to others. It's important to understand the public relations of your situation and what it means in the grand scale of things and frame it in such a way. When I taught at LAVC, I invited my co-worker Brian Sher, who was an ICM lit agent (now a manager) to speak. A student asked him, "I came in second place in the XYZ Screenwriting Contest, would you read my script?" His answer was, "No, but I'll read the first-place script." And be prepared should you win. Have another script ready to go, as the contacts you may meet as a result of winning the contest will probably ask, "What's next for you?" Being able to strike while the iron is hot and capitalize on the win is important. You can only ride the wave of success for a short time. When next year's winners are announced (or the winners of the next big contest), you are old news.

From entering your script to winning the contest, manage your expectations all along the way. Contests that promise introductions into the business, for example, cannot force agents to represent you or studios to buy your script. Enter contests with the knowledge that most of them need you more than you need them. A win might only be the first step on a very long journey to earning a living as a writer. Winning a contest is often an ephemeral high that, after enjoying whatever sizzle might come with it, probably won't advance you around the board even one square. Because you won the contest doesn't even mean the script is good. Yes, you won, but the nature of a contest is that someone must always win. Your winning screenplay might be the best of the worst—your turd didn't stink as badly as the other turds.

Because the likes of me have read so many contest-winning-scripts which have been disappointing or bad, we may not be as excited about your win as you are. And don't rely solely on contests as your point of entry into the business. You must still network and query, as much as you dislike it or as ineffective as it seems. Use a few contests annually as an adjunct to better writing and smarter networking. Accept the fact that contests are something of a vicious cycle for most writers. You might win a contest but the buzz will fade and you'll have to enter another contest and another and another and another and another year after year after year. The ironic thing is that whether a contest ever makes a difference is up to your writing, your screenplay, and you.

A comprehensive list of screenplay contests can be found on the Moviebytes website here: https://www.moviebytes.com/ and at ScriptReaderPro's website here: https://www.scriptreaderpro.com/screenwriters-calendar/. As Chris Lockhart points out, some contests are better than others. Here is a breakdown of the top contests that may be worth your time, and money, to enter:

The Top Screenwriting Contests

- Academy Nicholl Fellowship
- Austin Screenwriting Competition

Screenwriting Contests Also Worth Considering

- BlueCat Screenplay Competition
- Finish Line Script Competition
- Final Draft Big Break Contest
- PAGE International Screenwriting Awards
- ScreenCraft
- Scriptapalooza
- Scriptapalooza TV Contest
- Script Pipeline Screenwriting Contest
- Slamdance Screenplay Competition
- Sundance Screenwriters Lab
- Trackingb Feature and TV Script Contest
- Tracking Board Launch Pad

NETWORKING & WRITING GROUPS

It's not easy to make a living as a screenwriter. The odds can feel stacked against you, given the small size of the market and the competition from seasoned professionals. But every day, new writers enter the business. You need to really develop your craft, along with a thick skin and a serious work ethic, to succeed in this business. Networking in any business endeavor is critical, but doubly so in the film business. You may also need to move to Los Angeles, at least initially, if you're serious about getting your career off the ground, because that's where the business is. Many writers are wallflowers by nature, but you can and should learn to network. It takes time and practice, like anything else. Relationships are the coin of the realm in Hollywood, so cultivate as many as you can.

Because writing is such a solitary activity, it can also be helpful to have a supportive group of like-minded individuals to bounce ideas off, get script feedback from, and commiserate with about the challenges of being a scribe. Starting a writers' group can help you start and grow your network as well. For these reasons, many writers start their own writing groups. To start a writing group, find four or five like-minded writers and start meeting with them regularly, just to talk movies and screenwriting. It's important to meet regularly. As soon as you're comfortable with the makeup of the group, start meeting weekly, bi-weekly, or monthly to read and critique each other's works in progress. Pitch loglines to each other, share scenes or drafts of scripts you're working on. A good writing group can offer you an objective eye on your work, and it will keep you disciplined to write regularly. You can also join online writing groups or forums too. They're a little more impersonal, though. Whatever group you land with, make sure the makeup of the group has the right chemistry. Don't add people without a careful discussion amongst all the members, and don't let the group to get too big and unwieldy. The point of a writing group is to help focus all the members on the task at hand—writing screenplays.

Another way to network with other writers is to attend writing conferences or forums. If you're really committed and want to see your work produced, consider a screenwriting lab like the one run by the Sundance Institute in Utah. As their own website states: The Sundance Institute Feature Film Program supports "independent filmmakers from development through distribution" of their feature film projects. The program is over 30 years old now, and is considered a model for supporting artists. It operates by providing filmmakers mentorships, grants, and strategic support. Its goal is to foster "self-expression, risk-taking, collaboration, and community". The program has championed a number of first time independent feature filmmakers from around the world, and over 400 films supported by the program have been produced.

KEEP ON WRITING

If you're a writer, you'll keep writing no matter what. Those of us who have the bug, know it's a hard thing to shake. It's a part of you, and always will be. We write because we love writing. It brings us a unique pleasure that nothing else does. Most everyone who's ever spent any time working in the film business, especially as a writer, knows that success requires a combination of hard work and good luck. If you want to be a successful screenwriter, you have to keep working at your craft, and putting your work out there for others to judge. Most screenwriters spent decades writing before they found success. Stay true to yourself, and as long as you're getting some joy out of the work, keep at it. If the cards fall in your favor, you may succeed beyond your wildest dreams.

EXERCISES

Exercise 1: Start a writing group with two or three other students. Meet at least once every two weeks for starters to share ideas, loglines, and script pages.

Exercise 2: Enter your completed script in a writing contest.

Exercise 3: Research and compile a list of agents and managers who will read unsolicited scripts, then write a cover letter and query a few of them to see if they would be willing to read your script.

FURTHER READINGS/LISTENING:

The Hollywood Producers Directory by Jesse Douma and Dinah Perez, Esq.
Filmmakers and Financing by Louise Levison
How To Manage Your Agent: A Writer's Guide to Hollywood Representation by Chad Gervich
8 Differences Between Managers & Agents by Anna Klassen available at https://screencraft.org/2018/03/15/8-differences-between-managers-agents/
10 Things Smart Writers Do To Build a Screenwriting Career by Alex Simon, available at: http://www.scriptreaderpro.com/screenwriting-career-2/
Writers Group Therapy: Fighting Writer's Block and Other Literary Ailments available at: http://writersgrouptherapy.com/
Write Your Screenplay podcast by Jacob Krueger, available at https://soundcloud.com/jacob-krueger-studio

CPSIA information can be obtained
at www.ICGtesting.com
Printed in the USA
JSHW020232240720
6876JS00003B/10